Translation, Rewri and the Manipula Literary Fame

André Lefevere

Routledge
Taylor & Francis Group

LONDON AND NEW YORK

This edition reissued in the Routledge Translation Classics series 2017
by Routledge
2 Park Square, Milton Park, Abingdon, Oxon OX14 4RN

and by Routledge
711 Third Avenue, New York, NY 10017

Routledge is an imprint of the Taylor & Francis Group, an informa business

First edition published by Routledge 1992 as part of the Translation Studies
series, edited by Susan Bassnett and André Lefevere

British Library Cataloguing in Publication Data
A catalogue record for this book is available from the British Library

Library of Congress Cataloging-in-Publication Data
Names: Lefevere, Andrâe, author.
Title: Translation, rewriting, and the manipulation of literary fame / by
    Andrâe Lefevere ; preface by Scott Williams.
Description: Revised and enlarged. | Revised and enlarged edition has a new
    preface by Scott Williams. | Milton Park, Abingdon, Oxon ; New York,
    NY : Routledge, [2016] | Series: Routledge translation classics | Includes
    bibliographical references and index.
Identifiers: LCCN 2016028755 | ISBN 9781138208735 (hardback) |
    ISBN 9781138208742 (pbk.) | ISBN 9781315458496 (ebook)
Subjects: LCSH: Translating and interpreting. | Criticism, Textual. | Canon
    (Literature)
Classification: LCC PN241 .L364 2016 | DDC 418/.04—dc23
LC record available at https://lccn.loc.gov/2016028755

ISBN: 978-1-138-20873-5 (hbk)
ISBN: 978-1-138-20874-2 (pbk)
ISBN: 978-1-315-45849-6 (ebk)

Typeset in Times New Roman
by Apex CoVantage, LLC

Every effort has been made to contact copyright-holders. Please advise the
publisher of any errors or omissions, and these will be corrected in subsequent
editions.

Translation, Rewriting, and the Manipulation of Literary Fame

One of the first books to shine a light on the broad scope of translation studies, this *Routledge Translation Classic* is widely regarded as a pillar of the discipline. Authored by one of the most influential translation theorists of the twentieth century, *Translation, Rewriting, and the Manipulation of Literary Fame* shows how rewriting – translation, anthologization, historiography, criticism, editing – influences the reception and canonization of works of literature.

Firmly placing the production and reception of literature within the wider framework of a culture and its history, André Lefevere explores how rewriting manipulates works of literature to ideological and artistic ends, and demonstrates how rewriting a text can give it a new, sometimes subversive, historical or literary status.

Ranging across various literatures, including Classical Latin, French, and German, and here reissued with a new foreword by Scott G. Williams, this is a seminal text for all students and specialists in translation studies, literary theory, and comparative and world literature.

André Lefevere taught in the Department of Germanic Studies and Program for Comparative Literature at the University of Texas at Austin. He also co-edited the Routledge series *Translation Studies* with Susan Bassnett.

Contents

General editors' preface

2017

The growth of Translation Studies as a separate discipline is a success story of the 1980s. The subject has developed in many parts of the world and is clearly destined to continue developing well into the 21st century. Translation studies brings together work in a wide variety of fields, including linguistics, literary study, history, anthropology, psychology and economics. This series of books will reflect the breadth of work in Translation Studies and will enable readers to share in the exciting new developments that are taking place at the present time.

Translation is, of course, a rewriting of an original text. All rewritings, whatever their intention, reflect a certain ideology and a poetics and as such manipulate literature to function in a given society in a given way. Rewriting is manipulation, undertaken in the service of power, and in its positive aspect can help in the evolution of a literature and a society. Rewritings can introduce new concepts, new genres, new devices and the history of translation is the history also of literary innovation, of the shaping power of one culture upon another. But rewriting can also repress innovation, distort and contain, and in an age of ever increasing manipulation of all kinds, the study of the manipulation processes of literature as exemplified by translation can help us towards a greater awareness of the world in which we live.

Since this series of books on Translation Studies is the first of its kind, it will be concerned with its own genealogy. It will publish texts from the past that illustrate its concerns in the present, and will publish texts of a more theoretical nature immediately addressing those concerns, along with case studies illustrating manipulation through rewriting in various literatures. It will be comparative in nature and will range through many literary traditions both Western and non-Western. Through the concepts of rewriting and manipulation, this series aims to tackle the problem of ideology, change and power in literature and society and so assert the central function of translation as a shaping force.

Susan Bassnett
André Lefevere
1990

Foreword

The afterlife of a book

The act of reprinting evokes the afterlife of a book. Indeed, the choice to reprint it signals that the book has become more than what it was when first published. This is very much the case with *Translation, Rewriting, and the Manipulation of Literary Fame*. Surely, there will be many a reader who picks up a copy for the first time, but more likely than not that reader will come to it over a path others have trodden. In this marvelous and scary digital age, that path is quickly discerned. For instance, "Google Scholar" indicates that there are over 2,700 citations of the book. The books and articles that cite this title are in multiple languages with an amazing span of subject matter, including the translation of Chinese, Russian, Dutch, South African, English, German, Indian, Spanish, French, and classical Roman literature, not to mention film and other media. Through its emphasis on the power of rewriters, Lefevere's book illustrates the influence of multiple agencies in the dissemination of literature world-wide, anticipating issues relevant to contemporary research on world literature. Any history of modern Translation Studies will include reference to André Lefevere, and this is his most important book. In what follows, I wish to examine aspects of the (after)life of the book and the significance of the man who wrote it. I do not profess absolute objectivity because Lefevere was both friend and mentor to me, but I shall try my best to present the matter fairly.

Born in Belgium, André Alphons Lefevere got a Ph.D. from the University of Essex and then taught in Hong Kong and Antwerp before coming to the University of Texas at Austin. André Lefevere is a name widely known in Translation Studies circles. What some may not know is that he came to the University of Texas at Austin in 1984 as a professor for Netherlandic Studies and not Translation per se.[1] Indeed, he built up the Dutch program and even co-wrote his own beginning language textbook.[2] Throughout his tenure there, he taught everything from beginning language courses to graduate seminars. He also became active in the Comparative Literature program.[3] His graduate course in Comparative Literature on translation was, of course, quite popular.

If his seminar on translation inspired any of his students to learn more, and there were many, his door was always open. There would be students in Germanic Studies interested in translation and any number of Comparative Literature students coming in and out of his office. Whether they were interested in a European

language, Chinese literature, or some other part of the world, they all found something of value for their own project in conversations with him. One bookcase
in particular was full of books on translation. After some discussion, he would
stand up, walk to the bookcase, think for a moment and select one or two books.
Particularly with anthologies or collections of articles, he would take a pencil and
circle specific chapters in the table of contents. "Read these, come back and discuss them with me." Repeat. Sometimes a not so faint outline would betray that
he had chosen the same or different chapters for other students at some point in
the past. One day, peering over Lefevere's shoulder at the bookshelf, a graduate
student noticed a new looking book with Lefevere's own name on it: *Translation,
Rewriting, and the Manipulation of Literary Fame*. A different book, by someone
else, was in his hand, but he allowed me, that student, to take a copy of his book
with me as well. Just as the students who stepped across the threshold of his office
came from all over the world, just as his own career had taken him across oceans
and continents, the book shows a breadth of interests with case studies covering
different European cultures, ancient and modern, the Middle East, and Africa.
Also characteristic of the man is that he did not write it in jargon, rather in a way
that people not thoroughly versed in the debates among translation scholars could
understand.

   In Lefevere's book, translation is not merely a linguistic transfer but a cultural
process. Translation is another type of rewriting (along with, for instance, anthologies, historical books, criticism, etc.) motivated by the ideology and poetics of
people who hold some kind of power, or wish to use rewriting to gain power,
in the target culture (Lefevere discusses this as "patronage"). The ideology of a
given place and time in which the rewriting occurs combines with the dominant
poetological conceptions to determine the image of a work of literature that a
translation projects. Rewriters can create images not just of a work but also of a
writer, a genre, a whole period, etc. Although I did not yet know it at the time,
Lefevere's use of "systems" as a heuristic concept came in part from the influence
that the polysystems theory of Even-Zohar had had on many translation scholars.[4]
In Lefevere's thinking then, a "system" is both neutral and descriptive, designating
interrelated elements that share common characteristics, setting them apart from
other elements perceived as not belonging to the system. Many of Lefevere's ideas
connected directly or indirectly with what I had been learning about critical theory
in other Comparative Literature seminars, but I never thought to combine them or
apply them in this way to translation before taking Lefevere's seminar and reading
his book. In discussing the significant change of direction of Translation Studies
that occurred in the late 1970s, Susan Bassnett has written that, prior to this shift:
"To pass from a seminar on literary theory to a seminar on translation in those days
was to move from the end of the twentieth century to the 1930s." (1998: 124).
Like Bassnett herself, Lefevere was one of the major players to move the discourse about translation not only in a more fruitful direction for Translation Studies
but also into a position from which a dialogue with other disciplines was more
likely and, indeed, inevitable. In 1992, Routledge had published not only *Translation, Rewriting, and the Manipulation of Literary Fame* but also the source book

Translation, History, Culture that Lefevere had edited as a companion volume to it. If one also includes the many articles he wrote as well as the important work as co-author and editor of books on Translation Studies he did in collaboration with Susan Bassnett, Lefevere's output in the first half of the 1990s was tremendous. His work at the time seemed to resonate not just within Translation Studies but also with many literary and cultural studies scholars.

At about the same time as he published *Translation, Rewriting, and the Manipulation of Literary Fame*, Lefevere also published his *Translating Literature: Practice and Theory in a Comparative Literature Context* through the Modern Language Association (MLA). The connection between translation and Comparative Literature was very important in the early years as the field of Translation Studies began to establish itself as a distinct discipline. Lefevere helped to establish a strong awareness of Translation Studies among Comparative Literature departments and programs in the United States. In 1995, he edited a whole issue of the journal *Comparative Literature* on the topic of Translation. Two years after his death, in 1998, the American Comparative Literature Association (ACLA) met in Austin, Texas. The conference was held in memory of Lefevere, and its theme was "Literary and Cultural Translation and Exchange." We can see here the beginning of a long process that has gradually heightened the awareness of translation and the appreciation for its importance in literary studies. One can continue to see this process at work, for instance, in the fact that a decade later the conference theme of the Modern Language Association in 2009 was "The Tasks of Translation in the Global Context," and there was a special panel at the 2015 convention specifically conceived as a follow-up on that to discuss the evolving relationship between translation and the MLA. Two of the panel members were Catherine Porter, president of the MLA in 2009, and Sandra Bermann, who was the president of the ACLA in 2009. Together they had edited a companion to Translation Studies in 2014 with contributions by many of the leading Translation Studies scholars in the world. In the summer of 2016, the MLA hosted an international symposium entitled "Other Europes: Migrations, Translations, Transformations" in Düsseldorf, Germany. In 2011 the MLA adopted guidelines for peer review on evaluating translations as scholarship. This was an important step because many language and literature departments still regularly choose to ignore translation as a scholarly activity in evaluating its faculty for tenure and promotion. If translations themselves are of such little value, the study of them would be, too. Even as Translation Studies continues to strive in the United States to establish itself as an independent discipline, these links forged early on with other professional academic organizations have been crucial not only to the growth but to the very survival of the field in the United States. Although many people have, of course, been involved in this ongoing dialogue, Lefevere's ability to speak with such authority in both worlds was crucial in helping to establish the basis for these important relationships.[5]

Some translation scholars at the time looked more skeptically at Lefevere's *Translation, Rewriting, and the Manipulation of Literary Fame*. In a 1995 review of the book in the important Translation Studies journal *Target*, Hannah Amit-Kochavi notes that although it was published in a Translation Studies series, only "half of it deals directly with translation issues" (390). The brief review, as is not uncommon in the genre, focuses on what the reviewer considers wrong about the book and concludes rather curiously by stating that the book fails to consider "that no (inter)cultural contact, translation included, is possible without at least some adaptation of the material to be transferred to the current taste and values of the target culture" (390). This despite the fact that the whole book is about precisely how that very adaptation takes place. It does so effectively enough that people continue to read it and refer to it after more than two decades. A longer and more complex review was written by Theo Hermans (1994), himself an important figure in the early development of the field. The review covers not only *Translation, Rewriting, and the Manipulation of Literary Fame* but also two other titles by Lefevere, namely *Translation, History, Culture* and *Translating Literature: Practice and Theory in a Comparative Literature Context*. It then also tacks on a short discussion of a fourth title not from Lefevere (edited by Hardin, 1992). Hermans dedicates the lion's share of the review, however, to *Translation, Rewriting, and the Manipulation of Literary Fame*. Rhetorically the review is somewhat confusing as it alternates between praise and condemnation while Hermans elaborates on the latter almost to the exclusion of the former, nearly to the point that it can sometimes seem a little like reading Tacitus discuss Tiberius. Thus there are terms like "too rudimentary," "too apodictic," "too broad," "inconsistencies," "disturbing," "muddled," "naïve," "ineptly chosen," and "infuriating," to name a few. These stand in sharp contrast to, and often side by side with, other phrases like "refreshing and productive," "his work is of central importance to the discipline," "entirely sensible approach," "challenging and important." All this by someone "who essentially agrees with him." Furthermore, despite the negative rhetoric he employs in reviewing Lefevere's work, Hermans added a fourth title by someone else to the review evidently as a contrast in order to illustrate "just how much Lefevere has to offer."

Lefevere's shift from the term "refraction" (1982) to "rewriting" should not have surprised Hermans since he himself had edited a volume, *The Manipulation of Literature*, in 1985 that includes an article ("Why Waste our Time on Rewrites? The Trouble with Interpretation and the Role of Rewriting in an Alternative Paradigm") in which Lefevere not only begins to use the newer term but also outlines the ideas he would more thoroughly develop in *Translation, Rewriting, and the Manipulation of Literary Fame*. In an odd way, perhaps, Hermans was too close in his own thinking to Lefevere in order to appreciate the significance of the book outside of the inner-circle type debates that had gone on in those early years as the discipline was taking shape. Hermans states towards the end of the review that what Lefevere is trying to do is not "as new as he would have us believe," and again at the beginning: "Neither the overall approach nor the methodological tools which Lefevere offers are strikingly new, even if his particular emphasis on terms like 'ideology,' 'patronage,' and 'poetics' probably is." Of course, Lefevere had been developing these ideas over at least a decade, a process Hermans would have been following all too well. More than that though, Lefevere's thought process did not occur in a vacuum. However, it was precisely Lefevere's own "particular emphasis," his own unique interpretation of the whirlwind of ideas circulating in the same shared intellectual milieu that makes Lefevere, and the book being reprinted here, so important.

It may not have been the book that some of the other members of that same milieu wanted it to be, but the book that it actually was has had an impact far beyond that circle. For Amit-Kochavi, it could never be "a definitive textbook on its important subject." Of course, this is not a goal Lefevere ever claimed for the book. Instead, Lefevere treats it more like a prolegomenon: "This book is an attempt to emphasize both the importance of rewriting as the motor force behind literary evolution, and the necessity for further in-depth study of the phenomenon" (2). Whereas Hermans evidently wanted an entirely different book detailing theoretical concepts addressed to an inner circle, Lefevere wanted to address students as well as professionals: "Rewriting manipulates, and it is effective. All the more reason, then, to study it. In fact, the study of rewriting might even be of some relevance beyond the charmed circle of the educational institution . . . A study of rewriting will not tell students what to do; it might show them ways of not allowing other people to tell them what to do" (9). Lefevere had in mind an audience that went way beyond the current readership of a translation journal. Not only, though, did he succeed in that outreach, but despite the select criticism just after publication, his ideas continue to inspire and inform translation scholars. That continued interest as well as the the criticism constitute part of the afterlife of the book.

In his introductory book on Translation Studies, Jeremy Munday dedicates most of the chapter on "Cultural and Ideological Turns" to the discussion of Lefevere's book *Translation, Rewriting, and the Manipulation of Literary Fame* (191–214). Translation Studies readers (e.g. Venuti 239–255) might, however, include his much older article from 1982 "Mother Courage's Cucumbers: Text, System and Refraction in a Theory of Literature." The article maps out the categories of ideology and poetics that lay the groundwork for *Translation, Rewriting, and the Manipulation of Literary Fame*. In the book, however, Lefevere differentiates the concepts even more and illustrates the multiple factors that influence the manipulation in his various case studies. The article also introduces the idea of "refraction" which would later develop into "rewriting." One of the most quoted passages from *Translation, Rewriting, and the Manipulation of Literary Fame* refers to Lefevere's expansive concept of "rewriting:" "The same basic process of rewriting is at work in translation, historiography, anthologization, criticism, and editing" (9). Lefevere also references other forms of rewriting "such as adaptations for film and television" that he leaves out of the book itself because he felt they were outside his field of expertise. This concept of "rewriting" broadens the scope of the approach in such a way that even those not directly involved in Translation Studies before will take notice and find Lefevere's approach applicable across disciplines.

Lefevere, along with Bassnett, is most closely associated now with the cultural turn in Translation Studies. Cristina Marinetti notes that this approach shifted the focus away from linguistics and the notion of equivalence, maintaining instead that translation is a "fact of history and a product of the target culture" (2011: 26). Marinetti also points out that the shift of focus from language to culture enables the consideration of notions of power and discourse (2011: 26). Munday notes, too, that this focus on power relations provides an intersection between Translation Studies and Postcolonial Studies (203). Marinetti observes that the "recent turn to 'cultural translation' in sociology and to 'world literature' in Comparative Literature are further proof that the 'cultural turn' of the nineties was indeed innovative and almost prophetic in its tireless championing of translation as a vital concept that should become central to all disciplines involved in the study of cultural interaction" (2011: 30). In her book on comparative literature, first published in 1993, Bassnett had gone even further by declaring that Comparative Literature should be studied from within Translation Studies rather than the other way around (1998b: 161). This is something that both she and Lefevere proposed in the introduction to *Translation, History and Culture* in which they announced the "cultural turn" (1990: 12).

That announcement of the cultural turn by Bassnett and Lefevere may not have been the 'birth' of the approach but it was certainly its baptism, its naming day, so to speak. For years, scholars in different countries had sought alternatives to a limited linguistic approach to translation characterized by an emphasis on equivalence and prescriptive rules ideal for machine translation, the ideal of translation without involving those pesky humans. In *Translation, History and Culture*, Bassnett and Lefevere collected and published articles by many of these very people showing everyone else what was afoot and that the various contributions to the volume display "a remarkable unity of purpose" (1990: 4). Mary Snell-Hornby's own contribution discussed the situation in Germany, outlining in English what had been published chiefly or only in German at the time. For instance, she presented Vermeer's skopos theory and other culturally oriented German theorists. Snell-Hornby, in her 2006 book *The Turns of of Translation Studies,* discusses the development of the cultural turn throughout the 1980s. In reviewing the ideas of Vermeer, Reiss, Kade, Holz-Mänttäri and others, she traces the development in Germany of the importance of cultural factors leading to the functionalist approaches and the concept of translatorial action, before going on to the Brazilian "cannibalistic approach" and the influence of deconstruction (47–68). Given the many directions the field of Translation Studies has taken in the last twenty years, it is good to be reminded that these scholars felt engaged in a common enterprise. However, these and other similar approaches tend now to be dealt with separately in newer works about Translation Studies.[6]

Whether one reads Snell-Hornby's book, or any number of countless other books now in circulation about Translation Studies, one should remember the lessons of Lefevere about the power of a rewriter to create a new image.[7] Snell-Hornby, for instance, is considerably better disposed towards Lefevere's ideas than, say, Anthony Pym in his *Exploring Translation Theories*. Pym, too, is an important figure in contemporary Translation Studies, so I shall elaborate briefly on how he uses, and does not use, Lefevere's ideas so that I can make a point about the afterlife of Lefevere's *Translation, Rewriting, and the Manipulation of Literary Fame*. In a book organized largely around the effort to insert a reconsideration of equivalence back into translation theory, there is the very briefest mention of Bassnett and Lefevere in a whole chapter on Cultural Translation, namely only in a sentence stating that they were connected with the advocacy of the term "cultural turn" (366). References to Lefevere's book are also sparse and distributed between a chapter on the functionalists ("Purposes") and one on descriptive theories ("Descriptions"), but *not* in the chapter on Cultural Translation. In the chapter on the functionalists, there is brief mention of Lefevere's ideas comprising one of the few attempts to reconcile the concept of "function" as understood in systems theory, on the one hand, and in action theory, on the other. "One attempt might be André Lefevere's view of systems (1992), which includes factors very close to the translator (patrons, editors, publishers)" (187). Within a chapter on descriptive theories, there is a mention in a boxed section entitled "A shortlist of concepts in the descriptive paradigm" but with no further elaboration: "To understand not just translation but all kinds of 'rewriting,' we have to consider the social contexts, especially patronage (Lefevere)" (171–172). Later in the same section, under 'Sources and Further Reading', Pym writes: "A more entertaining approach to literary translation is André Lefevere's *Translation, Rewriting, and the Manipulation of Literary Fame* (1992)" (220). My purpose here is merely to point out that someone rewriting translation theory in a way that is unsympathetic to Lefevere's positions may downplay them, but would still be hard pressed to ignore Lefevere or his book completely.[8] If one wishes to pursue Translation Studies as it has developed over the latter half of the twentieth century into the twenty-first, one must engage with Lefevere and his ideas at some point.

It is difficult to know exactly what Lefevere would have produced over the the last twenty years had he lived or where his thinking would have taken him. Essays printed posthumously give some clue. He had, for instance, been working with the concepts of "grids" (both textual and conceptual)[9] and with the idea of texts as "cultural capital."[10] Lefevere was on a sabbatical when he passed away, during which he often used a separate office in the library at the University of Texas at Austin so that he could focus without interruption. He had checked out multiple volumes and anthologies of plays, arranged in several stacks in that office, and there lay still a notebook on the desk full of quotes and citations. One of the case studies in *Translation, Rewriting, and the Manipulation of Literary Fame* is on the *Lysistrata* by Aristophanes and one of his most famous articles had been on the translation of a play, *Mutter Courage*, by Brecht. He revisited the same Brecht play as an example of "cultural capital" in an essay published after his death. Lefevere examined how the interplay of three different types of rewritings (translation, criticism, and reference works) creates an image of a writer and text.[11] The notes in his office, however, show that he was looking at a much wider variety of plays translated from several languages. Susan Bassnett, with whom he regularly collaborated, is one of the pioneers in theorizing about theatre translation. Still today, it is one of the more understudied areas of Translation Studies. There have, however, been in the last few years several conferences and ever more articles and books not just on theatre translation,[12] but the relationship of performance and performativity to translation. What would Lefevere think of a "performance turn" in translation?

Since the publication of Lefevere's book, a great deal has happened in Translation Studies. For instance, there have been advances in the study of interpreting, localization, and also translation as it relates to various other media. Machine translation and translation software, too, have changed dramatically, and it is hard to think of a professional translation agency that does not use some sort of translation memory software. However, an algorithm based, for instance, on a database of usage is only as good as the data entered. Someone, some person, had to make a decision on what and how to translate at some point in order for there to be usable data for comparison. We are also, gradually, learning more and more about the way different cultures, not just in the West, have regarded translation and interpreting over the centuries (something Lefevere would have welcomed with open arms).[13]

There are multiple national and international organizations dedicated to translation. In the United States, Lefevere's adopted home, it is possible to get a degree in Translation Studies now. In addition to the American Translators Association (ATA) and the American Literary Translators Association (ALTA), there is now also the American Translation and Interpreting Studies Association (ATISA). The MLA and ACLA continue to have strong advocates for the study of translation. There is not, however, within the United States currently as close a dialogue between major figures in the field and all the various organizations as one might hope. As the discipline has grown, schools of thought have emerged with scholars eager to rewrite the profession in their own image. However, scholars can argue for their own ideas while also approaching the field with a "big tent" sensibility, acknowledging that all voices be heard, all theories and approaches discussed, not just within a single organization or discipline but across several. Here I will, appropriately, give Susan Bassnett the last word: "Translation is, after all, dialogic in its very nature, involving as it does more than one voice. The study of translation, like the study of culture, needs a plurality of voices." (1998: 138–139).

Scott G. Williams
Texas Christian University
Fort Worth, Texas

1   Prewrite

It is an amusement for me to take what Liberties I like with these Persians, who (as I think) are not Poets enough to frighten one from such excursions, and who really do want a little Art to shape them.

(Edward Fitzgerald xvi)

This book deals with those in the middle, the men and women who do not write literature, but rewrite it. It does so because they are, at present, responsible for the general reception and survival of works of literature among non-professional readers, who constitute the great majority of readers in our global culture, to at least the same, if not a greater extent than the writers themselves.

What is usually referred to as "the intrinsic value" of a work of literature plays much less of a part in this than is usually assumed. As is well known, the poetry of John Donne remained relatively unknown and unread from a few decades after his death until his rediscovery by T. S. Eliot and other modernists. Yet it is safe to assume that the "intrinsic value" of his poems must have been the same all along.

Similarly, many "forgotten" feminist classics originally published in the twenties, thirties, and forties of our century have been republished in the late seventies and eighties. The actual content of the novels was, presumably, no less feminist then than it is now, since we are dealing with exactly the same texts. The reason why the republished feminist classics are not forgotten all over again lies not in the intrinsic value of the texts themselves, or even the (possible) lack thereof, but in the fact that they are now being published against the background of an impressive array of feminist criticism, which advertises, incorporates, and supports them.

Whoever identifies the goal of literary studies as such with the interpretation of texts will either have no explanation for these phenomena, or else have somewhat embarrassed recourse to vague notions such as fate. It is my contention that the process resulting in the acceptance or rejection, canonization or non-canonization of literary works is dominated not by vague, but by very concrete factors that are relatively easy to discern as soon as one decides to look for them, that is as soon as one eschews interpretation as the core of literary studies and begins to address issues such as power, ideology, institution, and manipulation. As soon as one does this, one also realizes that rewriting in all its forms occupies a dominant position among the concrete factors just referred to. This book is an attempt to emphasize both the importance of rewriting as the motor force behind literary evolution, and the necessity for further in-depth study of the phenomenon.

Rewriters have always been with us, from the Greek slave who put together anthologies of the Greek classics to teach the children of his Roman masters, to the Renaissance scholar who collated various manuscripts and scraps of manuscripts to publish a more or less reliable edition of a Greek or Roman classic; from the seventeenth-century compilers of the first histories of Greek and Latin literature not to be written in either Greek or Latin, to the nineteenth-century critic expounding the sweetness and the light contained in works of classical or modern literature to an increasingly uninterested audience; from the twentieth-century translator trying to "bring the original across" cultures, as so many generations of translators tried before, to the twentieth-century compiler of "Reader's Guides" that provide quick reference to the authors and books that should have been read as part of the education of the non-professional reader, but go increasingly unread.

Their role has changed, though, and for two main reasons: the end of a period in at least Western civilization in which the book occupied a central position in both the teaching of writing and the transmission of values, and the split between "high" and "low" literature that began to take place toward roughly the middle of the nineteenth century, and led to a concomitant split between "high" and "low" writing about literature, "high" and "low" rewriting.

In his 1986 Presidential Address to the members of the Modern Language Association of America, J. Hillis Miller observed that "our common culture, however much we might wish it were not so, is less and less a book culture and more and more a culture of cinema, television, and popular music" (285a). Professional readers of literature (I use the term to designate both teachers and students of literature) recognize the development that is taking place, and they may privately react to this state of affairs with indignation, cynicism, or resignation, but the great majority among them continues to conduct business as usual, not least because the position they occupy within the institutions sheltering them leaves them very little choice indeed: degrees must be awarded, appointments made, tenure given, and promotions granted.

The fact that "high" literature is increasingly read only in an educational setting (both secondary and higher education), but does no longer constitute the preferred reading matter of the non-professional reader, has also increasingly limited the influence of the professional reader to educational institutions. No present-day critic can still claim the stature in society at large that was once enjoyed as a matter of course by, say, Matthew Arnold. Maybe the most obvious illustration of the contemporary isolation of both high literature and the study thereof has been provided by the vastly different impact of deconstruction on professional and non-professional readers. Whereas professional readers appear more or less convinced that deconstruction has, indeed, knocked away the very foundations of Western metaphysics, non-professional readers cannot be said to have paid overmuch attention to this momentous fact, certainly not nearly as much as they can be said to have paid to such mundane issues as health insurance and the stability of financial institutions.

If educational institutions increasingly function as a "reservation" where high literature, its readers, and its practitioners are allowed to roam in relative, though not necessarily relevant freedom, they also further contribute to the isolation of the professional reader. Professional readers need to publish in order to advance up the professional ladder, and the pressures of publication relentlessly lead to "the progressive trivialization of topics" that has indeed made the annual meetings of the Modern Language Association of America "a laughing stock in the national press" (Walter Jackson Bate quoted in Johnson 1). Needless to say, this "progressive trivialization" also serves to undermine further the professional reader's prestige outside the charmed circle drawn around him, or her, by educational institutions.

Yet within those institutions business does go on as usual, and it would appear that the majority of professional readers of literature has not yet grasped the paradoxical change that has taken place. Most professional readers of literature would not normally "stoop" to producing rewritings of the kind whose evolution through the centuries has been briefly charted above. They would see their "real" work as what non-professional readers would sorely be tempted to categorize under the heading of "progressive trivialization." That work, it is safe to state, hardly ever reaches the non-professional reader. Paradoxically, the only work produced within the charmed circle that still reaches that reader is precisely the type of rewriting most professional readers would tend to treat with a certain disdain. Yet the translation, editing, and anthologization of texts, the compilation of literary histories and reference works, and the production of the kind of criticism that still reaches out beyond the charmed circle, mostly in the guise of biographies and book reviews, no longer function as typically low-level activities within the wider framework of the interaction between professional and non-professional readers, between institutions of education and society at large. These types of rewriting used to be considered activities of a more "ancillary" kind. Yet by no means did they always play that role – witness the enormous impact of some translations, such as Luther's Bible translation, on both the literature and society of their time and beyond. Today, however, they have become the lifeline that more and more tenuously links "high" literature to the non-professional reader.

The non-professional reader increasingly does not read literature as written by its writers, but as rewritten by its rewriters. It has always been that way, but it has never appeared as obvious as it does today. In the past, too, many more people read the Authorized Version than read the Bible in its various original languages. Very few people had access to the actual manuscripts of the classics, and most readers were content, or had to be content with reading them in an edition. In fact, their trust was so great that they could occasionally be misled by convincing editions of non-existing manuscripts, as in the case of McPherson's *Ossian*. Byron and his generation did not read Goethe's *Faust* in German; but in the abbreviated

French version contained in Madame de Staël's best-selling *De l'Allemagne* (On Germany). Pushkin read the Byron he admired so much in French, not in English, and certainly not in Russian, a language he would speak only to his servants. Ezra Pound invented Chinese poetry for the West by means of an anthology of "translated" T'ang-dynasty poets, and Samuel Johnson obviously influenced the subsequent reception of the poets he included (and failed to include) in his *Lives of the English Poets.*

In the past, as in the present, rewriters created images of a writer, a work, a period, a genre, sometimes even a whole literature. These images existed side by side with the realities they competed with, but the images always tended to reach more people than the corresponding realities did, and they most certainly do so now. Yet the creation of these images and the impact they made has not often been studied in the past, and is still not the object of detailed study. This is all the more strange since the power wielded by these images, and therefore by their makers, is enormous. It becomes much less strange, though, if we take a moment to reflect that rewritings are produced in the service, or under the constraints, of certain ideological and/or poetological currents, and that such currents do not deem it to their advantage to draw attention to themselves as merely "one current among others." Rather, it is much more to their advantage to identify themselves quite simply with something less partisan, more prestigious, and altogether irreversible like "the course of history."

The non-professional reader of German literature, for instance, would have been extremely hard-pressed to find any poem by Heinrich Heine in anthologies of German poetry published between 1933 and 1945. In fact, the only poem by him that was included in those anthologies, the popular (too popular, in fact, to suppress) "Loreley," was labeled "anonymous." Obviously, whatever professional readers of German history put those anthologies together knew that it would not benefit their professional advancement to ascribe the poem to Heinrich Heine. It would benefit their professional advancement even less if, in an inexplicable attack of professional honesty, they would have stated in an introduction, or a footnote, why such a course of action would not have benefited their professional advancement. Histories of literature published at the same time would have told non-professional and professional readers alike, as Adolf Bartels did in his history of German literature, that "only Heine's vanity and arrogance were ever gigantic, and gigantic was the stupidity of the German people, that has for so long believed those who told it that he was one of their great writers" (335). As he proudly states in the preface to the 1943 edition of his history, Bartels was duly rewarded by the dominant ideological current: not only was he awarded the highest medal for achievement in the cultural field; he even received a personal congratulatory letter from Adolf Hitler on his birthday in that year.

Admittedly the example of Germany between 1933 and 1945 is somewhat extreme, as would be the example of the Eastern part of Germany between 1945 and 1989. Yet the existence of the image, and its previous construction, are the important point in all this. Images constructed by rewriters play just as important a part in societies more open in nature than those mentioned above; it's just that there are more images to choose from. If non-professional readers of literature were to be asked who Christopher Marlowe was, for instance, they are not likely to go and read Marlowe's collected works. Rather, they are likely to look up the name in a rewriting like the *Oxford Companion to English Literature.* If they need, or want to know more, they will probably consult some of the currently available histories of English literature. They might also call to mind productions of *Dr Faustus* for the stage or for the screen.

When non-professional readers of literature (and it should be clear by now that the term does not imply any value judgment whatsoever. It merely refers to the majority of readers in contemporary societies) say they have "read" a book, what they mean is that they have a certain image, a certain construct of that book in their heads. That construct is often loosely based on some selected passages of the actual text of the book in question (the passages included in anthologies used in secondary or university education, for instance), supplemented by other texts that rewrite the actual text in one way or another, such as plot summaries in literary histories or reference works, reviews in newspapers, magazines, or journals, some critical articles, performances on stage or screen, and, last but not least, translations.

Since non-professional readers of literature are, at present, exposed to literature more often by means of rewritings than by means of writings, and since rewritings can be shown to have had a not negligible impact on the evolution of literatures in the past, the study of rewritings should no longer be neglected. Those engaged in that study will have to ask themselves who rewrites, why, under what circumstances, for which audience. They owe what is probably one of the first statements of the "doctrine" of rewriting in Western literature to St Augustine. When faced with the fact that a fair number of pages in the Bible could, to put it mildly, not be said to correspond too closely to the kind of behavior the then still relatively young Christian Church expected from its members, he suggested that these passages should, quite simply, be interpreted, "rewritten," until they could be made to correspond to the teachings of the Church. If a scriptural passage, Augustine observed, "seems to commend either vice or crime or to condemn either utility or beneficence," that passage should be taken as "figurative" and "subjected to diligent scrutiny until an interpretation contributing to the reign of charity is produced" (93).

Augustine's situation is exemplary for that of all rewriters. He is obviously influenced by the fact that he occupies a certain position within a certain institution, as all rewriters are. Toward the end of his life he occupied a somewhat elevated position in an organization based on a certain ideology that had therefore a vested interest in preserving that ideology and in combating and destroying rival ideologies. Other rewriters would occupy positions at courts, in educational institutions, and in publishing houses.

If some rewritings are inspired by ideological motivations, or produced under ideological constraints, depending on whether rewriters find themselves in agreement with the dominant ideology of their time or not, other rewritings are inspired by poetological motivations, or produced under poetological constraints. When

Rufus Griswold published *The Poets and Poetry of America* in 1842 he stated in the preface that American poetry "is of the purest moral character" (Golding 289). He obviously wanted it to remain so and steadfastly refused to include later poets whose moral character he considered doubtful, such as Walt Whitman. His anthology therefore projected a slanted image, *but one that functioned as reality for generations of professional and non-professional readers alike.* Since it was widely read and since aspiring poets looked to it for models to emulate "it effectively controlled the moral and intellectual range of subject matter in canonical poetry" (Golding 289).

When W. B. Yeats wrote a "Memoir" of William Blake for the edition of that poet's works he produced together with Edwen Ellis, and which was published in 1893, he literally invented the following ancestry for Blake: "the grandfather of William Blake was an Irish aristocrat named John O'Neil who took the name of his wife, 'an unknown woman' and became 'Blake' to escape imprisonment for debt" (Dorfman 205). By giving Blake an Irish grandfather, and therefore a Celtic lineage, Yeats could link Blake to the "Celtic Twilight" that was so important to him at that particular stage of his own poetic development. Needless to say, the Blake "constructed" by Yeats and Ellis "functioned" as the "real" Blake for readers of the 1893 edition, even though Yeats also unabashedly rewrote lines of Blake's that he considered inferior.

One of the most striking examples of the combination of ideological and poetological motivations/constraints is the epigraph to this chapter, taken from a letter written by Edward Fitzgerald, the enormously popular Victorian rewriter of the Persian poet Omar Khayyam. In fact, Fitzgerald's *Rubayyat* is one of the most effective rewritings of the last century, and its influence makes itself felt deep into the present one. Ideologically Fitzgerald obviously thinks Persians inferior to their Victorian English counterparts, a frame of mind that allows him to rewrite them in a way in which he would have never dreamed of rewriting Homer, or Virgil. Poetologically he thinks they should be made to read more like the dominant current in the poetry of his own time.

Whether they produce translations, literary histories or their more compact spin-offs, reference works, anthologies, criticism, or editions, rewriters adapt, manipulate the originals they work with to some extent, usually to make them fit in with the dominant, or one of the dominant ideological and poetological currents of their time. Again, this may be most obvious in totalitarian societies, but different "interpretive communities" that exist in more open societies will influence the production of rewritings in similar ways. Madame de Staël, for instance, can be shown to have been rewritten in pro- or anti-Napoleon and pro- or anti-German terms during the French Second and Third Republics, which prided themselves on being among the most open societies of their time.

Rewriting manipulates, and it is effective. All the more reason, then, to study it. In fact, the study of rewriting might even be of some relevance beyond the charmed circle of the educational institution, a way to restore to a certain study of literature some of the more immediate social relevance the study of literature as a whole has lost. Students now "exist in the most manipulative culture human beings have ever experienced" (Scholes 15). Studying the processes involved in rewriting literature will not tell students how to live their lives (they are much more likely to turn to the screen for that kind of model), nor will it teach them to write well, the other traditional justification for the study of literature. But it might serve as some kind of model that enables them, to some extent, "to see through the manipulations of all sorts of texts in all sorts of media" (Scholes 15). A study of rewriting will not tell students what to do; it might show them ways of not allowing other people to tell them what to do.

The same basic process of rewriting is at work in translation, historiography, anthologization, criticism, and editing. It is obviously also at work in other forms of rewriting, such as adaptations for film and television, but these are outside of my area of expertise and will therefore not be dealt with here. Since translation is the most obviously recognizable type of rewriting, and since it is potentially the most influential because it is able to project the image of an author and/or a (series of) work(s) in another culture, lifting that author and/or those works beyond the boundaries of their culture of origin, four chapters of this book will be devoted to the study of translated literature. Four more will be devoted to each of the other main forms of rewriting. As a heuristic construct for the study of rewriting I shall make use of the concept of "system," first introduced into the domain of literary studies by the Russian Formalists, in the conviction that their models may indeed "provide a direction for future enquiry" (Morson 2). I have opted for this concept because its basic tenets are relatively easy to explain, which has a distinct pedagogical advantage; because it promises to be "productive" in the sense that it may reveal problems of importance to the study of rewriting that other heuristic constructs do not reveal; because it is "plausible" in the sense that it is also used in other disciplines, not just in literary studies, and to some advantage, which might also work against the growing isolation of literary studies within educational institutions; and because it provides a neutral, non-ethnocentric framework for the discussion of power and relationships shaped by power, which may benefit from a more dispassionate approach. I shall further introduce the concept of "system" in Chapter 2.

With Alastair Fowler I believe that "in the last resort literary theory is only as comprehensive and as penetrating as the reading it is based on" (quoted in Cohen xiii). I have therefore tried to build this book on readings taken from different literatures: classical Greek, Latin, French, and German. In doing so, I hope to have escaped "one irony of current theories of historical difference," which is that "they largely ignore different histories" (Morson 2). Finally, in an attempt to overcome provincialism in literary scholarship, I have extended my readings to cover Afro-English and Dutch literature. A fair number of examples have also been taken from Chinese, Arabic, and other non-Western literatures in an attempt to make this book free from the symptoms of literary provincialism "which are a widespread ignorance of non-Western literatures [and] an almost total ignorance of the smaller Western literatures" (Warnke 49). As a result, some of the material quoted is quoted in the guise of the most obvious rewriting of all: translation. All translations are my own.

At a time when career advancement and other institutional considerations tend to further, or even necessitate the production of "high" rewritings of literature in the very speculative manner practiced by various guru figures (many younger people in the profession are likely to be given tenure or promoted on the basis of publications written in a manner of discourse they themselves would be the first to banish from any composition classes they teach), I have constructed the argument of this book on the basis of evidence that can be documented, and is. Since some of this material is not likely to be familiar to the average reader of this type of book, I have had liberal recourse to quotations from sources generally regarded as authoritative.

2   The system: patronage

Poetrias ineditas
scribam tibi, si me ditas.
(Archipoeta 376)

The concept of system was introduced into modern literary theory by the Russian Formalists. They viewed a culture as

a complex "system of systems" composed of various subsystems such as literature, science, and technology. Within this general system, extraliterary phenomena relate to literature not in a piecemeal fashion but as an interplay among subsystems determined by the logic of the culture to which they belong.

(Steiner 112)

Some variants of sociological criticism, some criticism based on communications theory, and various strands of reader-response criticism have done much to create a climate in which it is once again possible to think about literature in terms of system. Recent attempts at elaborating a systems approach within literary studies have been undertaken by Claudio Guillen, Itamar Even-Zohar, Felix Vodička, and Siegfried J. Schmidt. Outside of literary studies the systems approach has mainly been championed in recent years by Niklas Luhmann, while Lyotard's *The Postmodern Condition* takes its bearings from "Parson's conception of society as a self-regulating system" (11).

Unfortunately, as Dieter Schwanitz points out: "A great obstacle to the reception of systems theory by literary scholars, however, is its forbidding level of abstraction" (290). This is certainly borne out in the case of both Luhmann and Schmidt. However, since the present book does not attempt to contribute to any further elaboration of General Systems Theory, but rather tries to make use of systems thinking as a heuristic construct, I shall merely introduce the main concepts of systems thinking and show how they can be applied to the study of rewritings in a productive manner.

When I use the word "system" in these pages, the term has nothing to do with "the System" (usually spelled with a capital S) as it increasingly occurs in collo-quial usage to refer to the more sinister aspects of the powers that be, and against which there is no recourse. Within systems thinking the term "system" has no such Kafkaesque overtones. It is rather intended to be a neutral, descriptive term, used to designate a set of interrelated elements that happen to share certain characteristics that set them apart from other elements perceived as not belonging to the system. "Literature," in Schmidt's words,

> can be analyzed as a complex social *system* of actions because it has a certain structure, an in-out differentiation, is accepted by society and fulfills functions which no other system in this society can fulfill.
>
> (563)

Literature – a literature – can be analyzed in systemic terms. Systems thinking would call it a "contrived" system, because it consists both of texts (objects) and human agents who read, write, and rewrite texts. Even though the educational system gives the impression, especially in the case of the classics, that texts generated by men and women of genius are suspended in some timeless vacuum for our further edification, "classic texts, while they may or may not originally have been written by geniuses, have certainly been written and rewritten by the generations of professors and critics who make their living by them" (Tompkins 37). The fact that literature is a contrived system should caution us against any attempt to force it into an analogy with physical or biological systems, which are amenable to a more rigid description.

Literature is not a deterministic system, not "something" that will "take over" and "run things," destroying the freedom of the individual reader, writer, and rewriter. This type of misconception can be traced back to the colloquial use of the term and must be dismissed as irrelevant. Rather, the system acts as a series of "constraints," in the fullest sense of the word, on the reader, writer, and rewriter. It is not my intention to give the impression that there is a ruthless, unprincipled, and excessively cunning band of translators, critics, historiographers, editors, and anthologists "out there," snickering as they systematically "betray" whichever work(s) of literature they are dealing with.

On the contrary, most rewriters of literature are usually meticulous, hard-work-ing, well-read, and as honest as is humanly possible. They just see what they are doing as obvious, the only way, even if that way has, historically, changed over the centuries. Translators, to lay the old adage to rest once and for all, have to be trai-tors, but most of the time they don't know it, and nearly all of the time they have no other choice, not as long as they remain within the boundaries of the culture that is theirs by birth or adoption – not, therefore, as long as they try to influence the evo-lution of that culture, which is an extremely logical thing for them to want to do.

What has been said about rewriters obviously also holds for writers. Both can choose to adapt to the system, to stay within the parameters delimited by its con-straints – and much of what is perceived as great literature does precisely that – or they may choose to oppose the system, to try to operate outside its constraints; for instance by reading works of literature in other than the received ways, by writing works of literature in ways that differ from those prescribed or deemed acceptable at a particular time in a particular place, or by rewriting works of literature in such a manner that they do not fit in with the dominant poetics or ideology of a given time and place.

Here, for instance, are the constraints Shakespeare had to deal with:

> Like any other royal subject he had to satisfy – or at least not displease – the sovereign and her court; the Queen, for good reason, was sensitive to any challenge to the legitimacy of the monarchy, and her word could put an end to Shakespeare's career, if not his life. He had also to avoid the censure of the London authorities, whose Puritanism militated against any dramatic production as decadent, superstitious frivolity, and who sought excuses to close the theatres. As a new kind of ideological entrepreneur still working within traditional patronage relations of literary production, Shakespeare had to keep favour with his court patron – in this case the powerful Lord Chamberlain – who afforded the company political protection, and, literally, licence to work; at the same time, he had to hold the interest of a broad public drawn from London's mercantile, artisanal and working classes.
>
> (Kavanagh 151)

Literature, to go back to the description of the Russian Formalist theorists, is one of the systems that constitute the "complex 'system of systems' " known as a culture. Alternatively, a culture, a society is the environment of a literary system. The literary system and the other systems belonging to the social system as such are open to each other: they influence each other. According to the Formalists, they interact in an "interplay among subsystems determined by the logic of the culture to which they belong." But who controls the "logic of the culture"?

There appears to be a double control factor that sees to it that the literary system does not fall too far out of step with the other subsystems society consists of. One control factor belongs squarely within the literary system; the other is to be found outside of that system. The first factor tries to control the literary system from the inside within the parameters set by the second factor. In concrete terms, the first factor is represented by the "professional," who is

> felt to "render a service" rather than provide an ordinary commodity, and it is a service that he alone, qua professional, can supply. The latter aspect of professionalism lends its practitioners their peculiar authority and status: they are regarded as possessing a monopoly of competence in their particular "field."
>
> (Weber 25)

Inside the literary system the professionals are the critics, reviewers, teachers, translators. They will occasionally repress certain works of literature that are all too blatantly opposed to the dominant concept of what literature should (be allowed to) be – its poetics – and of what society should (be allowed to) be – ideology. But they will much more frequently rewrite works of literature until they are deemed acceptable to the poetics and the ideology of a certain time and place much as Karl Gutzkow, for instance, rewrote Georg Büchner's *Dantons Tod* "because such things as Büchner had flung down on paper, the kind of expressions he allowed himself to use, cannot be printed today" (84). Furthermore, Gutzkow did so because he did not want to "give the censor the pleasure of striking passages" (84). Trespassing on the turf of a fellow professional, he therefore "performed the office" (84) himself. In other words, because he wanted *Dantons Tod* to be read and because Büchner himself opposed both the dominant poetics and the dominant ideology, Gutzkow adapted the text to the point where it became acceptable to that poetics and that ideology. The writer chose to oppose the constraints; the rewriter to adapt to them.

The second control factor, which operates mostly outside the literary system as such, will be called "patronage" here, and it will be understood to mean something like the powers (persons, institutions) that can further or hinder the reading, writing, and rewriting of literature. It is important to understand "power" here in the Foucauldian sense, not just, or even primarily, as a repressive force. Rather:

> what makes power hold good, what makes it accepted, is simply the fact that it doesn't only weigh on us as a force that says no, but that it traverses and produces things, it induces pleasure, forms knowledge, produces discourse.
>
> (Foucault 119)

Patronage is usually more interested in the ideology of literature than in its poetics, and it could be said that the patron "delegates authority" to the professional where poetics is concerned.

Patronage can be exerted by persons, such as the Medici, Maecenas, or Louis XIV, and also by groups of persons, a religious body, a political party, a social class, a royal court, publishers, and, last but not least, the media, both newspapers and magazines and larger television corporations. Patrons try to regulate the relationship between the literary system and the other systems, which, together, make up a society, a culture. As a rule they operate by means of institutions set up to regulate, if not the writing of literature, at least its distribution: academies, censorship bureaus, critical journals, and, by far the most important, the educational establishment. Professionals who represent the "reigning orthodoxy" at any given time in the development of a literary system are close to the ideology of patrons dominating that phase in the history of the social system in which the literary system is embedded. In fact, the patron(s) count on these professionals to bring the literary system in line with their own ideology:

> In thus smoothing out contradiction, closing the text, criticism becomes the accomplice of ideology. Having created a canon of acceptable texts, criticism then provides them with acceptable interpretations, thus effectively censoring away elements in them which come into collision with the dominant ideology.
>
> (Belsey 109)

Patronage basically consists of three elements that can be seen to interact in various combinations. There is an ideological component, which acts as a constraint on the choice and development of both form and subject matter. Needless to say, "ideology" is taken here in a sense not limited to the political sphere; rather, "Ideology would seem to be that grillwork of form, convention, and belief which orders our actions" (Jameson 107). There is also an economic component: the patron sees to it that writers and rewriters are able to make a living, by giving them a pension or appointing them to some office. Chaucer, for instance, successively acted as "the King's envoy, the controller of customs on wool, hides and sheepskins, [and] the subforester of North Petherton" (Bennett 1:5). Chaucer's contemporary, John Gower, on the other hand, was his own patron, at least in this respect, being "an independent country gentleman, whose means allowed him to write in Latin, French and English" (Bennett 1:6). Yet he was not independent on the ideological level: he wrote his *Confessio Amantis* at the request of Richard II, and he "wrote a final passage praising the King. Some years later, the poet found it expedient to omit this passage, and to insert a new preface, praising Henry IV" (Bennett 1:6).

Patrons also pay royalties on the sale of books or they employ professionals as teachers and reviewers. Finally, there is also an element of status involved. Acceptance of patronage implies integration into a certain support group and its lifestyle, whether the recipient is Tasso at the court of Ferrara, the Beat poets gathering around the City Lights bookstore in San Francisco, Adolf Bartels proudly proclaiming that he has been decorated by Adolf Hitler, or the medieval Latin Archipoeta, who supplied the epigraph to this chapter, which reads, rewritten in English: "I shall write unheard of poems for you, if you give me wealth."

Patronage can be differentiated or undifferentiated, or rather, literary systems can be controlled by a type of patronage that is either differentiated or undifferentiated in nature. Patronage is undifferentiated when its three components, the ideological, the economic, and the status components, are all dispensed by one and the same patron, as has been the case in most literary systems in the past in which an absolute ruler, for instance, would attach a writer to his or her court and give him or her a pension, and as is the case in contemporary totalitarian states where, though the court has gone – at least in the sense in which I have used the word here – subventions and pensions remain.

Patronage is differentiated, on the other hand, when economic success is relatively independent of ideological factors, and does not necessarily bring status with it, at least not in the eyes of the self-styled literary elite. Most authors of contemporary bestsellers illustrate this point rather well.

In systems with undifferentiated patronage, the patron's efforts will primarily be directed at preserving the stability of the social system as a whole, and the literary production that is accepted and actively promoted within that social system will have to further that aim or, at the very least, not actively oppose "the authoritative myths of a given cultural formation" (White x) which those in power want to control because their power is based on them. This is not to say that there will be no "other" literature produced within that social system, only that it will be called "dissident," or any name to that effect, and once it has been written it will experience great difficulty in getting published through official channels, or else it will be relegated to the status of "low" or "popular" literature.

As a result, a situation of *de facto* literary diglossia tends to arise, as has been the case in many literary systems with undifferentiated patronage, in which literature as such is unquestioningly equated with the production of a more or less small, more or less large coterie operating within the orbit of the patronage group that is in power. The Ottoman Empire, for instance, produced a coterie literature centered on the court of Istanbul and closely modeled on classical Arabic examples, whereas the literature produced in the country at large, modeled on Turkish traditions, was never taken seriously by the coterie group and always rejected as "popular" if referred to at all. This same "popular" literature was to become "elevated" to the position of a national literature after the change of patronage produced by Kemal Atatürk's revolution.

In certain instances the pressure against being considered popular was so great that writers themselves preferred to restrict the circulation of their work to other members of the coterie only. Tudor English literature is a case in point. Writers dependent on the patronage of the court ran the risk of forfeiting that patronage, at least in part, if their work was seen to enjoy too much popularity with the masses in the streets. Hence the somewhat paradoxical situation, to our way of thinking at least, in which writers who had the printing press at their disposal for the dissemination of their work actually refused to have their books printed, and certainly not in large editions, preferring to circulate them in manuscript among other members of the coterie, known as persons of taste and discernment, rather than to abandon them to the vulgar crowd. The latter tended to find its reading matter in the continuations of medieval romances and other bestsellers, the kind of literature that has hardly survived in the literary histories of our time, which often only take the production of the coterie into account. The refusal to publish even subsisted for a considerable period of time after the Tudors: "Hence it was that practically nothing of Donne's verse was printed before 1633, two years after his death, although twenty-five manuscripts containing poems by him, and which circulated during his lifetime, survive" (Bennett 3:193).

Acceptance of patronage implies that writers and rewriters work within the parameters set by their patrons and that they should be willing and able to legitimize both the status and the power of those patrons as attested most forcibly, for instance, by the African praise song, a collection of honorific epithets commemorating and celebrating the patron's great and noble deeds, or by the panegyric in the Islamic system, which served mainly the same purpose, or by the many odes written to Comrade J. Stalin, or maybe, somewhat less forcibly so, by Pindar's great odes. An even subtler form of the same phenomenon can be observed in pre-eighteenth-century India, where "many poets even went so far as to allow their patron to claim the authorship of their work, or at least to help him in his literary endeavors, which would explain why one encounters a disproportionate number of royal writers in Indian literature" (Glasenapp 192).

Present-day developments in the literary system as it exists in Europe and the Americas show that undifferentiated patronage need not be based mainly on ideology as it was in most literary systems in the past. The economic component, the profit motive, may well lead to the re-establishment of a system with a relatively undifferentiated patronage, as attested by:

> The growth of large chains of retail bookstores, the strong rivalry of paperback publishers for rack space in retail outlets, the computerization of inventory and warehouse systems, the arrival on the scene of a new breed of literary agent, the influence of television talk shows that regularly feature authors as guests, the control by entertainment conglomerates of hard cover and paperback publishing companies and the like, and the increasingly active involvement of Hollywood in the business of book publishing.
>
> (Whiteside 66)

Institutions enforce or, at least, try to enforce the dominant poetics of a period by using it as the yardstick against which current production is measured. Accordingly, certain works of literature will be elevated to the level of "classics" within a relatively short time after publication, while others are rejected, some to reach the exalted position of a classic later, when the dominant poetics has changed. Significantly, though, works of literature canonized more than five centuries ago tend to remain secure in their position, no matter how often the dominant poetics itself is subject to change. This is a clear indication of the conservative bias of the system itself and also of the power of rewriting, since while the work of literature itself remains canonized, the "received" interpretation, or even the "right" interpretation in systems with undifferentiated patronage, quite simply changes. In other words, the work is rewritten to bring it in line with the "new" dominant poetics.

A large-scale example of this process is provided by the reconstitution of the canons of various national literatures after the socialist revolutions in Eastern Europe and the Soviet Union. A comparison of authors who have been canonized in the Federal Republic of Germany and the German Democratic Republic since the end of the Second World War is likely to yield two rather different lists. Yet the further back one goes in time, the more the lists overlap. The works of literature canonized will be the same, but the rewritings by means of which they are presented to the audience differ, sometimes radically. It is quite common for the classics to be presented as suited to different ideologies and poetics as these succeed each other, indeed to be pressed into the service thereof. Works of literature written long enough ago can therefore "boast" a whole concatenation of contradictory rewritings.

The conservative tendency of the literary system, any literary system, becomes even more of an issue in the countries mentioned above when the problem of deciding which new works can safely be admitted to the canon has to be addressed. Since the dominant poetics unabashedly subscribes to "realism" and is therefore all but squarely rooted in the nineteenth century, and since this poetics is intended to be used as a yardstick for measuring literature produced in the twentieth century, tension and conflict are all but inevitable.

If a certain type of institution, such as academies or influential literary journals and recognized publishers of highbrow literature, which have increasingly taken over the part played by academies in the past, play an important part in admitting new works to the canon, other institutions, such as universities and the educational establishment in general, keep the canon more or less alive, mainly by means of the selection of texts for literature courses. To put it in a nutshell, the classics taught will be the classics that remain in print, and therefore the classics that remain in print will be the classics known to the majority of people exposed to education in most contemporary societies.

The selection process also operates within the entire oeuvre of a certain author commonly regarded as a classic. Certain books by certain authors that are the staple of courses in institutions of (higher) education will be widely available, whereas other works written by the same author will be very hard to find except in painstakingly collected editions on library shelves. In the English-speaking world, for instance, Thomas Mann's *Doctor Faustus* and *The Magic Mountain* are widely available at the time of writing, *Buddenbrooks* somewhat less so, and *Joseph and His Brothers* hardly at all, even though the latter work was translated – rewritten – into English and published soon after it came out in German, as were all of Mann's other books.

It would only be a small exaggeration to say that in the present state of the educational system in both the United Kingdom and the United States the reading lists designed for examinations for Master of Arts and Doctor of Philosophy reflect rather accurately the canon of the present historical period. It lists not just the English and American writers who are considered worthy of study and emulation, but also those writers from other literatures or, perhaps more accurately, those books written by writers in other literatures that are allowed into the British and American systems because they are acceptable to the various ideologies and poetics currently dominating those systems. In other words, most of the highbrow literature in the United Kingdom and certainly in the United States is kept alive – somewhat artificially – by means of reading lists designed for institutions of (higher) education, which, in turn, guarantee a substantial turnover for the paperback lists of institutions publishing books.

The conservative influence of educational institutions on the literary system has perhaps nowhere been more apparent than in the Islamic system where poets had for a long time "learned their art exclusively through personal interaction with their predecessors" (Gibb and Landau 80). However, when philological schools were established, first in Basra and then in other cities, poets began to be taught by philologists, with obvious results:

> poets approached their art more or less philologically and accepted philological criteria for poetic value, especially with reference to the ostensibly unreachable superiority of pre-Islamic poetry. This development is probably much more responsible for the formalization of Arabic literature in the following centuries than any other single factor.

(Gibb and Landau 81)

(Potential) canonization greatly influences the availability of a work of literature. Candidates for canonization, not to mention canonized authors themselves, will much more easily be published by influential publishing houses (or by "licensed" publishing houses in systems with undifferentiated patronage), while works of literature which differ relatively sharply from the dominant ideology and/or poetics of the time will have to make do with *samizdat* in one form or other or with publication in another literary system. Many Black and Colored South African writers, for instance, have had their work first published in English in East European countries, particularly the German Democratic Republic.

What goes against the grain may also ostensibly be published outside the system, though with the more or less openly avowed intention of operating within that system. In eighteenth-century France, for instance, many potentially subversive works of literature (and philosophy) were routinely said to have been published in Amsterdam or Strassburg, that is, outside of the domain of the power of the literary system and the jurisdiction of the political system they set out to challenge.

Canonization appears at its most obvious and also at its most powerful with the spread of higher education. It has found its most impressive – and most profitable – monument to date in the publication of that hybrid crystallization of the close and lucrative cooperation between publishers and institutions of higher education: the introductory anthology (for use in Poetry, Drama, or Fiction 101) which offers a cross-section of canonized texts prefaced by a short exposition of the poetics that ensured their canonization. Works of literature are taken out of their historical context and the whole genealogy of influences and rewritings of which they are a part is silently obliterated. As a result, what has survived this process appears to be timeless, and what is timeless should, obviously, not be questioned.

The inbuilt conservative weighting of institutions of patronage can also be observed in the influence they exert on those who become involved with them, especially those who were previously of an anti-institutional or avant-garde cast of mind. Writers who achieve a remarkable, or even potentially disturbing impact with their first (few) works find themselves gradually absorbed into the mainstream, paradoxically because they have been able to introduce a new element into the dominant poetics or because they have been able to propose a novel function for literature, or both, as in the case of Bertolt Brecht.

Once their innovations begin to be accepted and imitated by other writers, soon to be labeled "epigones" in supplements to literary histories, a bandwagon effect is created that more or less effectively neutralizes the disturbing aspect in the novelty of their work. *Mother Courage* produced in 1989, for instance, looks quite different from the *Mother Courage* produced twenty or even forty years ago, and through no fault of the author. Indeed, the writers themselves simply live on and work as honored mentors, often achieving in life the very opposite of what they set out to achieve in art.

Educational institutions and their programs often leave a rather conservative imprint on the imagination of individual authors. It is instructive in this respect to compare the manifestoes authors write (in which they often argue the case for change) with the actual work they produce to illustrate those manifestoes. That work usually proves to be much closer to the work of the canonized authors who were part and parcel of the "rebel's" education. Joachim du Bellay, author of the *Défense et illustration de la langue française,* is a case in point. His "manifesto" is usually regarded as the harbinger of the "new" French Renaissance poetry as practiced by the poets of the Pléiade. To illustrate the poetics he advocated, du Bellay produced three cycles of lyrical poetry: *Les Antiquités de Rome, Olive,* and *Les Regrets,* all three "based to a large extent on his own Latin poetry" (Forster 30). What was touted as "new" within the French system did, in fact, turn out to be a rewriting of a rewriting of works of literature du Bellay had been exposed to as part of his education.

Change in a literary system is also closely connected with patronage. Change is a function of the need felt in the environment of a literary system for that system to be or remain functional. In other words, the literary system is supposed to have an impact on the environment by means of the works it produces, or the rewritings thereof. If these expectations are not met, or even consistently frustrated, patrons are likely to demand or, at least, actively encourage the production of works of literature more likely to meet their expectations: "the necessity to increase the arousal potential of aesthetic products over time inexorably comes down to a pressure to increase novelty, incongruity and other collative variables" (Martindale 232).

In systems with differentiated patronage the result is the increasing fragmentation of the reading public into a relative profusion of subgroups. In systems with undifferentiated patronage, on the other hand, readers' expectations are more restricted in scope and the "right" interpretation of various works tends to be emphasized by means of various types of rewriting. In the fourth and fifth centuries of the Common Era rewriting was applied on a large scale to classical Greek and Latin literature, basically to allegorize it to such an extent in the service of the newly dominant ideology of Christianity that it would become acceptable to the new patrons and thus escape destruction. Odysseus on his voyage home, it was shown, "really" represented the soul on its pilgrimage to heaven, and the "divine child" evoked by Virgil in his fifth eclogue, merely meant to celebrate an impending happy event in the family of Augustus, which subsequently failed to materialize, was unerringly identified with Christ himself. The latter rewriting was largely responsible for Virgil's enhanced status as a proto-Christian all through the Middle Ages, as is evident from his selection as Dante's guide in the first two books of the *Commedia.* A corresponding Marxist allegorization has been applied to writers of the nineteenth century by critics like Georg Lukács, who persisted in claiming that Balzac, say, was "objectively" a progressive social analyst and social commentator even though relatively few readers would, admittedly, be able to see this on the mere surface of his work, which had obviously been waiting for the "right" interpretation.

If a literary system resists change altogether, it is likely to collapse under growing pressure from its environment as soon as a differentiation of patronage sets in, usually under social conditions analogous to those prevailing in the West European Enlightenment state, or when a certain type of patronage is superseded by another one, radically different in nature. Of all literary systems known in history the classical Chinese system has been able to resist change the longest, precisely because undifferentiated patronage limited both the producers and the readers of literature to a relatively small coterie dominated by the court and the mandarins, and also because it could impose its ideology and its poetics by making them a (sizable) part of the requirements to be met by those who wanted to belong to that coterie.

Even those who never passed the imperial examinations, eking out a meager living as recluses or vagabonds, continued to write in terms of the dominant ideology and the dominant poetics because they had to rely, at least to a certain extent, on the charity of their former classmates or other mandarins glad to be able to enjoy the company of cultured gentlemen (even though their appearance might ostensibly belie that fact) while sitting out their stints in remote provinces.

This state of affairs could – and did – continue only as long as the environment was itself relatively homogeneous and secure. The literary system kept producing works of literature in a language no longer spoken by the majority of the population and with little or no bearing on what was actually happening in the environment. When that environment came under increasing pressure from outside and when new groups, capable of offering alternative sources of patronage, such as the emerging bourgeoisie, began to appear inside it, the literary system crumbled very rapidly, being also undermined from within by a large number of rewritings, namely translations of Western works of literature, in most cases through the intermediary of Japanese, which supplied the models for a new poetics.

3   The system: poetics

Rien n'appartient à rien, tout appartient à tous.
Il faut être ignorant comme un maître d'école
Pour se flatter de dire une seule parole
Que personne ici-bas n'ait pu dire avant vous.

[Nothing belongs to nothing, all things belong to all.
Ignorant as a schoolmaster must you be called
To flatter yourself that you have said one single word
Nobody else did not say before you on this earth.]
(Alfred de Musset 421)

A poetics can be said to consist of two components: one is an inventory of literary devices, genres, motifs, prototypical characters and situations, and symbols; the other a concept of what the role of literature is, or should be, in the social system as a whole. The latter concept is influential in the selection of themes that must be relevant to the social system if the work of literature is to be noticed at all. In its formative phase a poetics reflects both the devices and the "functional view" of the literary production dominant in a literary system when its poetics was first codified.

Once a poetics is codified, it exerts a tremendous system-conforming influence on the further development of a literary system. In Earl Miner's words:

> A systematic poetics emerges in a culture after a literary system proper has been generated and when important critical conceptions are based on a then flourishing or normatively considered genre. The coinciding of major critics with the considered genre generates the critical system. It is because Plato and Aristotle took drama as the norm that they considered imitation the essential character of literature.

(350)

And since they did so, they proceeded to develop a critical vocabulary to describe the drama, many of whose terms are still in current use in most European languages, even though they came into being in classical Greek more than two thousand years ago.

The functional component of a poetics is obviously closely tied to ideological influences from outside the sphere of the poetics as such, and generated by ideological forces in the environment of the literary system. In traditional African literature, for instance, with its emphasis on the community and its values, literature was not supposed to be conducive to personal fame. In fact, all traditional African literature is, by Western standards, "anonymous" and classified under the name of the tribe (the community), not that of the individual, the author, who remains unknown.

Practice precedes theory when the poetics of a literary system is codified. Codification occurs at a certain time, and this implies both the selection of certain types of current practice and the exclusion of others. The codification of a poetics is the work of literary professionals, though not necessarily of the type we now more or less automatically associate with that term. Codification did occur in traditional African literature, that is the literatures of sub-Saharan Africa as they developed from about the beginning of the Common Era to the advent of the White man and beyond, but the lack of written records in the African system prevented the rise of a group of literary professionals in the Western sense. It did not, however (a sobering thought indeed), prevent the production of literature as such. In literary systems that rely on the spoken, not the written word, criticism is probably at its most direct and its most effective: the artist whose performance is not considered acceptable is simply told to stop then and there, and dismissed without any form of remuneration.

"Important critical conceptions" do not find explicit expression in all literary systems. They do not in the African system, even though they are most certainly at work within it, and probably to the highest degree. Literary systems that rely on the spoken word tend to be much more rigid and conservative than literary systems that rely on the written word, simply because there is no opportunity to "go back and check" at a later time: once the word is spoken, it is gone. The community will therefore see to it that words are spoken, tales told, and poems composed in the "right" way, the more so since literary works produced within these systems also tend to incorporate what would lead a separate existence as "historical texts" in systems that rely on writing. In literary systems that rely on the spoken word, works of literature are intricately bound up with the identity of the community as such.

Nor are "important critical conceptions" explicitly formulated in the Chinese and Japanese literary systems, or at least not in the way readers of Western literature would expect them to be. In the formative stages of both the Chinese and the Japanese systems these critical conceptions were not written out in discursive prose or verse, but rather implicitly contained in anthologies, such as the *Shih Ching* and the *Chu Tzu* in the Chinese system or the *Manyoshu* and the *Kokinshu* in its Japanese counterpart. The process of codification is probably more apparent in those systems in which teaching relied more on written example than on precept, than in systems in which codification took the form of discursive prose or verse, codifying varieties of existing practice mainly by abstracting their "rules" and prescribing these rules for future writers to follow. These "rules" are preserved in the kind of textbook poetics familiar in the Indian, Islamic, and, especially, Western literary systems. Yet the codification of a poetics did take place in both cases, and in both cases it came about through the intermediary process of rewriting.

Codification of a poetics also entails the canonization of the output of certain writers whose work is regarded as conforming most closely to the codified poetics. The work of those writers is then propagated as an example for future writers to follow, and it occupies a central position in the teaching of literature. Rewritings tend to play at least as important a part in the establishment of the poetics of a literary system as original writings do. The two "professionals" who are responsible for establishing the canon of classical Greek literature, as it still stands today, are two relatively unknown librarians who lived in Alexandria in the third century before the Common Era: Aristophanes of Byzantium and Aristarchus of Samothrace. They both worked in the great library of Alexandria, and the classifications they drew up in the course of their cataloguing work proved to be of immeasurable importance, not just in anointing "classical" writers, but also in delineating genres.

Similarly, in the Islamic system, the *mu allakat,* the original pre-Islamic canon consisting of seven *qasidahs,* could hardly have achieved the status they now enjoy through the efforts only of the poets who composed them. Canonization was at least as much the result of the efforts of the *rawis* or apprentice poets who began to learn their trade as professional reciters and spread the fame of the masters to whom they were apprenticed.

In systems with differentiated patronage, different critical schools will try to elaborate different canons of their own, and each of these schools will try to establish its own canon as the only "real" one, meaning the one corresponding to its poetics, its ideology, or both. One of the most recent and influential examples of the process has been described as follows:

> With breathtaking boldness *Scrutiny* redrew the map of English literature in ways from which criticism has never quite recovered. The main thoroughfares on this map ran through Chaucer, Shakespeare, Jonson, the Jacobeans and Metaphysicals, Bunyan, Pope, Samuel Johnson, Blake, Wordsworth, Keats, Austen, George Eliot, Hopkins, Henry James, Joseph Conrad and D. H. Lawrence. This *was* "English literature."
>
> (Eagleton 32)

Not surprisingly " 'English' included two and a half women, counting Emily Brontë as a marginal case; almost all of its authors were conservatives" (Eagleton 33).

F. R. Leavis, the rewriter of the canon of English literature, was able to propagate his canon through teaching at Cambridge; T. S. Eliot, who was elaborating his own canon of English and world literature at about the same time, did not have a similar institutional base. Indeed, he failed to see "[T]he importance of the educational system as an agency of cultural continuity. As a result of this failure, he proved incapable of carrying through any sustained cultural project of wider scope than the tiny readership of the *Criterion*" (Baldick 131) – the journal he himself had started. Far from failing in his turn, Leavis went on to become the most influential British critic of his generation, turning generations of students into devoted Leavisites.

Codification takes place at a certain time, and once it has taken place the poetics of a literary system tends to take on a life of its own, increasingly divorced from later developments in the environment of the literary system. The Islamic *qasidah*, for instance, codified at a time when poets, like their fellow tribesmen, traveled frequently through the desert begins – according to the rules that had not yet been collected in a book – with the poet riding through the desert and spotting the remains of an old camp site. He is deeply moved by this, because the place reminds him of an old love affair, a battle that once took place there, or a hunt he took part in nearby. Later on, when the actual style of living had changed completely in the environment of the literary system, "this introduction will remain mandatory, even when the poets are no longer familiar with deserts or camp sites, battles or the hunt" (Abd el Jalil 32).

Change in the poetics of a literary system very rarely occurs at the same pace as change in the environment of that system. Sonnets were written when the horse was the fastest means of transportation, and they are still being written, albeit with slight modification, in the age of jet travel. Similarly, European poetics underwent a fundamental change from Antiquity to the Middle Ages and back again to the Renaissance. Plato and Aristotle took drama as the norm and therefore considered imitation the essential functional feature of their poetics. But the Middle Ages knew very little drama in that sense. Isidore of Seville, the author of one of the earliest medieval poetics, imagined that "drama" meant that the author read his text aloud while mimes acted out what he was reading – an interesting, though somewhat naive attempt at reconciling the precepts of a poetics with the facts observable in the environment of the literary system of which he was a part. In other words, he tried to reconcile what he read in his manuscripts with what he could see out of his window.

The medieval literature that originated in Provence and owed nothing to Aristotle was based on lyrical poetry, not drama. It was to become the basis of the whole medieval system of European literature, which accounts for the fact that the basic tenets of Western medieval poetics are much closer to the fundamental concepts of non-Western literary systems, in which the lyric happened to be the dominant genre at the time of codification and consequently influenced the important critical conceptions of literary systems in which drama would appear much later, if at all.

The boundaries of a poetics transcend languages, and ethnic and political entities. This fact is perhaps most convincingly demonstrated by the traditional African literary system, in which a common poetics was shared by more than four thousand languages south of the Sahara. The communities sharing this poetics were, moreover, living in a wide variety of forms of social and political organization, ranging from the San bands of hunters and food-gatherers of South Africa to independent villages and kingdoms or empires marked by a high degree of centralization, in some of which the literary artist even had the option of becoming a professional. Yet, by and large, both the inventory and the functional components of African poetics are common to traditional Zulu literature in the south of Africa, Yoruba literature in the north-west, Acoli literature in the northeast, Bakongo literature in the center, and Merina literature on the island of Madagascar. The situation is different in Egypt and the Maghreb because they belong to the Islamic rather than the African system.

The Islamic system itself also demonstrates the futility of any attempt at confining literature to a given language, even though it may be convenient to refer to particular systems in this way. Rather, the real boundaries of literary systems tend to be drawn by their common ideology, often extended through conquest or imposed by authority, or by a succession of ideologies social systems have evolved or are able to accommodate simultaneously. As far as its inventory component is concerned (its functional component did undergo slight modifications), the poetics of the Islamic system is the poetics evolved in Arabia and based on works of literature composed in Arabic.

As Islam spread outwards from Arabia, that poetics was adopted by other languages, and other ethnic and political entities. A poetics "suited" to Arabic, a Semitic language, was successively taken over by Persian, an Indo-European language, which contributed a new genre, the *roba'i* (rewritten in English as "quatrain"), by Turkish, a Finno-Ugrian language, and by Urdu, a mixture of Persian and Hindi. In the process the poetics was not "bent" to "suit" each language; precisely the opposite happened, no matter what the effect on each language was to be. That effect was especially marked in Turkish. When that language "adapted itself to the Arabic-Persian metrical forms, it did violence to its own nature, since it is a language unsuited to quantitative meters" (Bombaci 48).

This last statement points to a similarity with the Western system that is not easy to overlook. Indeed, the analogy between the Islamic and European systems is rather striking, as soon as one is prepared to see it. In both cases, a poetics is codified in a certain language (Greek, Arabic) and then adapted in other languages (Latin, the vernacular languages of Europe, Persian, Turkish, Urdu) without there ever existing a political unit encompassing all those languages, at least not for more than a few centuries, and, in both cases, the poetics transcends the boundaries of individual languages. There are local variations in both cases, to be sure, but the general picture is clear. The European poetics was later exported across the Atlantic and survived there for a relatively long time in a different environment without undergoing much notable change.

The reason why relatively few readers of this book can "see" the similarity between the European and the Islamic systems is intricately related to a development in the functional component of European poetics that occurred about a hundred and fifty years ago. Romanticism, itself a brilliant example of the way in which a poetics transcends languages, and ethnic and political entities, insists that language does indeed represent the dominant feature of a literary work, or that a literature is circumscribed by the language in which it is produced. This may, paradoxically, hold true for literary systems the Romantic critics most definitely did not have in mind, such as the Chinese and Japanese systems, but compared to other literary systems these constitute the exception rather than the rule.

Romanticism has been extremely successful in projecting its own functional component back in time, thus effectively "monolingualizing" literary histories, producing histories of German, French, and English literature usually devoted in large part to historical periods in which literature was produced on German, French, and English soil in different languages (one of them usually Latin) and according to the prescriptions of a shared poetics.

Romanticism's strategy of projecting its own functional component back in time has perhaps been most successful in the formulation – as part of the inventory component of its poetics – of the doctrine of the "three basic genres": "the" lyric, "the" epic, and "the" drama. The strategy itself is a brilliant illustration of the successful usurpation of traditional authority by a "new" school:

> One does not easily refrain from projecting on the founding text of classical poetics a fundamental articulation of "modern" poetics – which, in fact, and this will often be the case – turns out to be *romantic* – and maybe not without detrimental theoretical consequences, for by usurping this distant filiation, the relatively recent theory of the "three basic genres" not only attributes to itself an age it does not have and, by doing so, an appearance or presumption of eternity and hence of being obvious.
>
> (Genette 8)

The following examples offer further evidence of the fact that a poetics is not circumscribed by a language. The poetics of the literatures produced in the various Indo-European languages spoken on the Indian subcontinent remain remarkably similar, even though the languages themselves have progressively grown further apart. The same holds true for the literatures produced in the Dravidian languages of southern India and Sri Lanka. In Hellenistic literature a number of writers with different geographical origins and, to some extent, different mother tongues all conformed to Greek poetics, a trend that would continue in the literature of the Roman Empire, in which the rules of that poetics were followed in both Greek and Latin. Similarly, Provençal literature was composed in a language which was never actually spoken. Speakers of different variants, or different languages (Italians and Moors writing in Provençal) would conform to that language, and they would go on conforming to the poetics of Provençal in the various languages of medieval Europe, with the exception of English. Finally, in the formative stage of the Japanese literary system, literature was not produced in Japanese, but in Chinese. Chinese poetics was to occupy a position in the further development of the Japanese literary system that appears highly analogous to the position occupied by Latin in the European Middle Ages. It should, therefore, be "clear at once that there is such a thing as the tradition of the composition of texts, and that that tradition is completely independent of the tradition of speaking according to a certain matrix that has been handed down historically, i.e. independent of historically developed individual languages" (Coseriu 40).

The inventory component of the poetics of a literary system is not immediately subject to direct influence from the environment once the formative stage of the system is past. The functional component is more likely to undergo direct influence from outside the system. This influence tends to find its most obvious expression in the themes written about in various stages of the system. A theme linked to the rise of the novel in the European system, for instance, is that of the virtuous young heroine persecuted by the wicked aristocrat, seduced and abandoned. About a century later, the working-class heroine succeeds her middle-class sister when the wicked aristocrat is joined in the ranks of the depraved by the wicked bourgeois employer. Developments in the environment of the literary system, such as the relative loosening of strict moral dictates and the increasing availability of birth-control devices, have since contributed to robbing the theme of much of its topical interest. In fact, it tends to surface in contemporary literature mainly in comedy, or as parody.

Particular themes tend to dominate certain periods in the evolution of a system: the vanity of all things and the obsession with death in the European baroque, for instance, or industrialization in the European nineteenth century, at least in prose. Poetry, being more conservative, admitted the theme on a comparable scale only some fifty years later. In non-Western literary systems, *the* main theme from the sixteenth century onwards has been the challenge represented by Western ways.

Themes and, to a lesser extent, the functional component of a poetics exert an innovative influence on the literary system as a whole, whereas the inventory component of the poetics tends to exert a more conservative influence, which also affects the way in which a theme can be treated.

> A writer may claim, like Sidney, to look in his heart and write but he will actually, like Sidney, see his heart only through the formal perspectives open to him. In *Astrophel and Stella* the Petrarchan sonnet sequence provided Sidney with the occasion to look into his heart, and lent its coloring to the picture of Stella he found there.
>
> (Scholes 130)

The conservative influence exerted by the inventory component of a poetics is also attested by the fact that genres seem to be able to lead a shadowy existence as "theoretical possibilities" when not actively practiced and that they can be revived sooner or later. Genres tend to dominate certain stages in the evolution of a literary system (the *tanka,* for instance, succeeded by the *renga* and the *haiku* in Japanese literature) only to be relegated to a more secondary role that does not exclude the possibility of rediscovery and new use.

Romanticism did, broadly speaking, administer the final blow to the epic, whereas the Renaissance cast out the ballad as unacceptable and reinstated the epic after a period of almost twelve hundred years during which no work of literature had been written that corresponded to the Renaissance concept of what an epic ought to be. In contemporary literature both the epic and the ballad continue to be written, even though the epic in its post-Pound avatar has moved further away from its historical predecessor than the ballad.

A poetics, any poetics, is a historical variable: it is not absolute. In a literary system the poetics dominant today is quite different from the poetics dominant at the inception of the system. Its functional component is likely to have changed, and its inventory component will have changed as well, in most cases. Yet every poetics tends to posit itself as absolute, to dismiss its predecessors (which amounts, in practice, to integrating them into itself) and to deny its own transience or, rather, to see itself as the necessary outcome of a process of growth of which it happens to be the best and therefore also the final stage. Each dominant poetics freezes or certainly controls the dynamics of the system. It achieves this goal more easily in systems with undifferentiated patronage.

To retain its "absolute" position as long as possible, a poetics must deny or, at least, rewrite the history of the literature it dominates at a given time. The most notorious recent examples of this process can be plucked at random from that period in German literature in which a poetics closely linked with the Nazi ideology occupied the dominant position in the literary system. "Julius Petersen's reclaiming of Goethe for the Hitler Youth" is one such example among many, as is the description of Schiller as "Hitler's comrade in arms" (Eibl 29). In another, wider context this process can be seen at work in the struggle that took place in nearly all non-Western systems in the nineteenth century: the struggle between the traditional poetics intent on keeping the system closed to Western influence and a new poetics trying to strike a balance between the traditional and the imported, which is perceived as either potentially liberating or potentially subversive depending on the ideological position taken.

Finally, a changeable and changing poetics, established mainly by means of rewritings, will also dictate which original works of literature and which rewritings are acceptable in a given system, or, rather, such a poetics will be the touchstone used by teachers, critics, and others to decide what is in and what is out. As such that poetics will exert a tremendous influence on the interpenetration of two literary systems. In most cases the dictates of the poetics are ahistorical, witness the translation of poetry in the European (and American) system. The poetics of that system has long dictated that poetry should be translated into rhyming, metrical verse, quite oblivious of the fact that the poetry of its own formative period, the poetry written in classical Greek and in Latin, did not rhyme at all and, even though metrical, was written in meters different from those used in the literature of successor languages. The rhyme and meter rule, which reigned supreme until about the outbreak of the Great War, has been responsible for the failure of many a translation to carry its original across into the Western system. This situation, in turn, greatly obstructed the process of assimilation.

Different poetics dominant at different stages in the evolution of a literary system will judge both writings and rewritings in different, irreconcilable ways, all based on good faith and the conviction that each is the representative of the only truth. Let us look, for instance, at the reviews of Ezra Pound's *Homage to Sextus Propertius*. Pound's rewriting was damned by Professor Wilson Hale of Yale University, who quite obviously based his judgment on the then valid criteria – based on the then dominant poetics – for evaluating a translation. It was defended by those arguing the case for a different poetics. A. R. Orage wrote:

> With some of Professor Hale's literal criticisms it is impossible not to agree. Speaking in the name of the schools, he is frequently correct. But in the name of the humanities, of life, of art, of literature, what does it matter that Mr. Pound has spelled Punic with a capital when he meant a small letter.
>
> (in Homberger 158)

Nearly twenty years later James Laughlin argued that Pound's rewriting had been judged on the basis of the wrong poetological *criteria: "it has occurred to me that Variations on a Theme of Propertius'* would be a more accurate title than *Homage to Sextus Propertius.* It is sometimes as hard to locate Propertius' figure in Pound's recreation of it as it is to detect Haendel's theme in Brahms' variations on it" (quoted in Homberger 322).

Pound's early shorter poems can also be seen as an illustration of the way in which different poetics react to the same work of literature through the pen of different critics. First of all, it is significant that "none of the established American magazines, such as *Scribner's* or the *Century,* would publish the poems he submitted" (Homberger 2). In 1911 Charles Granville asserted the then dominant poetics against the newcomer:

> We need not attempt the very difficult task of defining poetry; but we can at least enunciate two or three qualities whose presence is necessary in all poetic compositions:
> (1) Poetry is born of the emotions. A true poet is capable of imposing his own emotion upon hearer and reader.
> (2) The expression of the reader's emotion must be in rhythmic and beautiful language.
> (3) The language must be characterized by perspicuity, for the sole reason that the emotion is not conveyable to reader or hearer unless it be clearly expressed.
>
> (quoted in Homberger 78)

A review based on a poetics of this nature could hardly be favorable to Pound's early work which was, as another reviewer subscribing to the same poetics, R. M. Allen, observed: "guiltless of form, as form is known to masters or students of the art of poetry" (quoted in Homberger 100). Rupert Brooke deplored that Pound had "fallen, it appears, under the dangerous influence of Whitman, and [he] writes many poems in unmetrical sprawling lengths that, in his hands, have nothing to commend them" (quoted in Homberger 59). Precisely this feature endeared Pound's early work to F. S. Flint, then also struggling to evolve an alternative poetics, who wrote: "one thing is proved by these two little books of his, *Personae* and *Exultations,* and that is that the old devices of regular metrical beat and regular rhyming are worn out" (quoted in Homberger 65).

It would be easy to conclude, somewhat philosophically, that history proved Pound and Flint right and the others wrong. History does not prove anything. History is made by people, according to certain constraints that are, it is claimed in this book, mainly systemic in nature.

Once a literary system is established, it tends to try to reach and maintain a "steady state," as all systems do, a state in which all elements are in equilibrium with each other and with their environment. Strictly regulated systems even appoint individuals to institutions expressly created to bring that state of affairs into being, such as the Académie Française and other academies. Yet there are two factors, in the literary system as in all other systems, that tend to counteract this development. Systems develop according to the principle of polarity, which holds that every system eventually evolves its own countersystem, the way Romantic poetics, for instance, eventually stood neoclassical poetics on its head, and according to the principle of periodicity, which holds that all systems are liable to change. The evolution of a literary system is the complex interplay between the desire to reach a steady state, the two opposing tendencies just mentioned, and the way in which the social system's regulatory component (patronage) tries to handle these opposing tendencies.

Rewritten literature plays a vital part in this evolution. The struggle between rival poetics is often initiated by writers, but fought and won or lost by rewriters. Rewritings are also a perfect gauge to measure the extent to which a poetics has been interiorized. When Houdard De la Motte, for instance, "translates" the Iliad in such a way that half of it is left out – as will be shown in Chapter 7 – he does so in perfect good faith. Like many of his contemporaries he is absolutely convinced of the superiority of the poetics of which he is a representative and proceeds to act on the basis of this conviction, ruthlessly excising every aspect of Homer that could not be rewritten in terms of both *goût,* taste, and a poetics that regarded the *tragédie* as the pinnacle of literary achievement.

Rewritings, mainly translations, deeply affect the interpenetration of literary systems, not just by projecting the image of one writer or work in another literature or by failing to do so – as will be shown in Chapter 6 – but also by introducing new devices into the inventory component of a poetics and paving the way to changes in its functional component. The ode, for instance, became a fixture of the French literary system at the time of the Pléiade, via translations from the Latin. An analogous situation had occurred in Italy a little earlier where the ode, also inspired by translations from the Latin, had immediately assumed the place occupied by the *canzone* in the late medieval poetics. Moralizing translations, often influenced by the Jesuits, bent the picaresque novel into the shape of the *Bildungsroman.* The characteristic alternation of masculine and feminine rhymes was introduced into French poetry by Octavien de St Gelais's translations of Ovid and was only later taken up again by Ronsard. The sonnet was introduced into Chinese in the 1920s, through translations made by Feng Chi. The hexameter was introduced into German by the Homer translations of Johann Heinrich Voss. John Hookham Frere's translations of Pulci introduced ottava rima into English, where it was soon to be used by Byron in his *Don Juan.* Yet Goethe's pious "hope that literary history will plainly state who was the first to take this road in spite of so many obstacles" (39) remains exactly that.

Literary histories, as they have been written until recently, have had little or no time for translations, since for the literary historian translation has had to do with "language" only, not with literature – another outgrowth of the "monolingualization" of literary history by Romantic historiographers intent on creating "national" literatures preferably as uncontaminated as possible by foreign influences. Yet on every level of the translation process, it can be shown that, if linguistic considerations enter into conflict with considerations of an ideological and/or poetological nature, the latter tend to win out.

A. W. Schlegel's fateful pronouncement that "one of the first principles of the art of translation is that, for as far as the nature of a language allows, a poem should be recreated in the same meter" (52), which has been responsible for all kinds of metrical contortions in many translations produced between 1830 and 1930, was obviously not made on linguistic grounds. Browning's insistence on the "use of certain allowable constructions which, happening to be out of daily favour, are all the more appropriate to archaic workmanship" (1095) is responsible for the fact that most Victorian translations of the classics of Antiquity read so monotonously alike. It was not inspired by any linguistic necessity but by the desire to acquire the timeless through use of the archaic.

Even the creation of words bears out the same proposition. When the early Christians needed to translate the Greek word *musterion,* they did not want simply to Latinize it, because it was too close to the vocabulary used by the "mystery cults," Christianity's main competitor at the time. For the same reason they rejected words like *sacra, arcana, initia,* which would have been semantically acceptable. They settled for *sacramentum* because it was a term both neutral and close to the original. But when St Jerome wrote the Vulgate translation of the Bible, Christianity had won the battle against the mystery religions and he felt free to simply Latinize *musterion* into *mysterium* (cf. Klopsch 37–8). Similarly, the Aramaic Jesus Christ is supposed to have spoken did not have a copula. He can therefore never have said: "This is my body" when pointing at a loaf of bread. The copula was put in by translators for ideological rather than linguistic reasons.

4   Translation: the categories

Lifelines, noses, legs, handles: the *Lysistrata* of Aristophanes

Two factors basically determine the image of a work of literature as projected by a translation. These two factors are, in order of importance, the translator's ideology (whether he/she willingly embraces it, or whether it is imposed on him/her as a constraint by some form of patronage) and the poetics dominant in the receiving literature at the time the translation is made. The ideology dictates the basic strategy the translator is going to use and therefore also dictates solutions to problems concerned with both the "universe of discourse" expressed in the original (objects, concepts, customs belonging to the world that was familiar to the writer of the original) and the language the original itself is expressed in.

At the end of Aristophanes' *Lysistrata,* the heroine asks "Peace," an allegorical character played by a naked young lady of great beauty, to bring the Spartan peace emissaries to her, and she adds the line "En mē dido tēn cheira, tēs sathēs age" (line 1119 in Coulon and van Daele). The line translates literally as: if he doesn't give you his hand, take him by the – what is in the 1968 reprint of Liddell and Scott's famous *Greek-English Lexicon* still translated by means of the Latin phrase, *membrum virile* – the penis, in other words. Since the way these and other *membra* can be referred to in literature is to no small extent indicative of the ideology dominant at a certain time in a certain society, this may be as good a point as any to enter in *medias res.*

Patrick Dickinson translates the line quoted above as: "But if they *won't*/Give you their hands, take them and tow them, *politely,*/By their . . . life-lines" (118). Sixty-eight years earlier William James Hickie, who translated Aristophanes for the Bohn Classical Library, rendered the same line as: "If any do not give his hand, lead him by the nose" (442). Hickie is fond of noses in this connection, witness his translation of "kou mē tot alle sou kuon ton orcheon labetai" [lest not any other of the dogs grab you by the testicles] (line 363) as "And no other bitch shall ever lay hold of your nose" (405). He goes on to explain in a footnote: "meaning that she would anticipate such a casualty by pulling it off" (405). He then proceeds to shore up his interpretation of the line in a somewhat incongruous manner, by quoting Droysen's German translation of it: "doch sollte bei den Hoden dann kein Koeter mehr dich packen" [then no dog should take you by the testicles again] (405).

Fifty-nine years after Hickie, Sutherland translated the same line as: "If he won't give his hand, then lead him by the prick" (43). Three years later Parker translated: "If hands are refused, conduct them by the handle" (78). Ten years earlier Fitts wrote: "Take them by the hand, women/or by anything else if they seem unwilling" (51), and twenty years before that Way had written: "If they don't give a hand, a leg will do" (49). We could keep going, and there is no lack of passages in Aristophanes that could keep us entertained in a similar manner as we shake our heads over so many different translations. But the point should have been made by now.

It has been made perhaps most succinctly by Gilbert Seldes in the foreword to his *Lysistrata.* He points out that Aristophanes' comedy has been performed "as a propagandistic work for both pacifism and the rights of women, as an operetta and as a typical sexual comedy quite in the French manner" (ix). The play, to coin a phrase, "allows for many interpretations," including the interpretation of merely rendering it in as literal a translation as possible. What concerns me here, though, is the "simple" fact that the interpretations quite literally become the play for those who are unable to read the original or, in other words, that the translation projects a certain image of the play in the service of a certain ideology.

This fact is most apparent in the passages various translators insert in their translations, passages that are most emphatically not in the original. Seldes himself added a passage for the chorus that allows a group of senators to air their views on the interminable war:

> Chorus of Senators: We owe all to the war. The war must go on.
> First Senator: For if the war ends, all the laws we have passed, emergency measures to keep us in power, will become null and void and we'll have to go back to the work that we did, which wouldn't be pleasant.
>
> (27)

It is not particularly hard to guess that the following insert could not possibly have been written by Aristophanes himself, *and* that it must have been inserted for a purpose:

> Small particles of earth become a pot
> That's change and growth; the formless given form;
> And then it's fired and finished in the flame.
> Out of the chaos and the formlessness
> Of senseless war, of tribe with tribe, we'll mould
> With delicate skill a whole Nigeria.
> (Harrison and Simmons 40)

The insert is taken from a translation/adaptation, in short: a rewriting of Aristophanes' *Lysistrata* published in Ibadan, Nigeria, before, not after the Biafran war.

Similarly, the following insert can easily be linked to the cause (the ideology) that made a certain translator adopt a certain strategy in 1911:

> For here is a Cause to your hand
> More holy than any before:

And in it lies beauty, and wisdom,
And courage, and love of your land.
Nay, surely the mothers who bore you,
The silent mothers of yore,
They also were made of this metal,
And out of the bed of the nettle,
Wherein they bred you of old,
They, too, who spake not a word,
They, too, brave hearts, could have told
Their tale of wrongs unheard.
So forward I bid you, nor fail,
Nor yield what ye hold in your hand:
For the wind which now blows in your sail
Shall bear you to land.

                              (Housman 44)

It will come as no surprise that the translation containing this extract was published by The Women's Press during the heyday of the suffragette movement in Britain.

Since Aristophanic comedy is rather radical in attacking certain ideologies and defending others, most of the translators whose "Lysistratas" have been published over the past century and a half have felt the need to state their own ideology. Most of the translators whose work was published during the first half of that century and a half would agree with A. S. Way's statement: "the indecency of Attic comedy, which is all-pervading, which crops up in every play, and in the most unexpected places, is a sad stumbling-block to the reader, and a grievous embarrassment to the translator" (xix). While most of these translators fervently disagreed with an ideology that condoned this indecency, few went as far as the first translator of Aristophanes during the past century and a half, C. A. Wheelwright, who stated in his introduction that "The *Lysistrata* bears so evil a character that we must make but fugitive mention of it, like persons passing over hot embers" (62). In his translation he simply omits the very crux of the play: the oath the women take at the formal start of their sex strike. Furthermore, he simply ends his translation at line 827 of the original, refusing to translate lines 828 to 1215, one quarter of the play, not because he had suddenly forgotten all his Greek, but because his ideology was incompatible with the one expressed in Greek by Aristophanes.

Most other translators have tried to make *Lysistrata* fit their ideology by using all kinds of manipulative techniques. All of their strategies have been adequately described by Jack Lindsay in the introduction to his translation. Their "effort," he points out, "is always to show that the parts considered offensive are not the actual expression of the poet, that they are dictated externally" (15). Thus J. P. Maine states in his 1909 introduction that "Athens was now under an oligarchy, and no references to politics was [sic] possible, so Aristophanes tries to make up indecency [sic]" (1:x-xi). In his introduction written in 1820 and reprinted in 1909, in the second volume edited by Maine, John Hookham Frere states that "Aristophanes, it must be recollected, was often under the necessity of addressing himself exclusively to the lower class" (2:xxvi). Both Maine and Hookham Frere blame patronage for Aristophanes' woes, but each blames a completely different type of patronage. Two years later Benjamin Bickley Rogers writes that "in truth this very coarseness, so repulsive to ourselves, so amusing to an Athenian audience, was introduced, it is impossible to doubt, for the express purpose of counterbalancing the extreme gravity and earnestness of the play" (x). In this case Aristophanes is portrayed not as the sovereign author, but as the conscientious craftsman who has no other choice than to bow to the demands of his craft, and nothing will prevent (some) readers from wanting to feel that Aristophanes the man would not have done what Aristophanes the craftsman had to do.

It was left to A. S. Way, twenty-three years later, to express the translator's dilemma in the most delicately wordy manner:

> The *traduttore,* then, who would not willingly be a *traditore,* may not exscind or alter, but he may well so translate, where possible, that, while the (incorruptible) scholar has the stern satisfaction of finding that nothing has been shirked, the reader who does not know the Greek may pass unsuspectingly over not a few unsavoury spots – not that his utmost endeavours can make his author suitable for reading (aloud) in a ladies' school.
>
> (xx)

The translator is caught between his adherence to an ideology that is not that of Aristophanes, indeed views sexual matters in a quite different manner, and his status as a professional who must be able to convince other professionals that he is worthy of that title, while at the same time not producing a text that runs counter to his ideology.

Yet ideology is not the only factor to determine the translator's strategy. Poetics is another. Some early translators, in fact, use Aristophanes' poetics as an argument to defend him against the ideological charge of indecency. Wheelwright, for instance, states that Aristophanes

> works occasionally with unclean tools and . . . chastises vice by open exposure of its turpitude, offending the ear whilst he aims to mend the heart. This fashion of plain speaking was that in which he wrote, and the audience demanded and would have it. If we cannot entirely defend the indelicacy of his muse, we cannot deny that a great share of the blame rests with the spectators.
>
> (ix)

In other words, Aristophanes could not have written otherwise, even if he had wanted to, and the translator can ease his own conscience and that of his readers by strongly implying that Aristophanes would have wanted to if only he had been allowed to. The constraints imposed by patronage and poetics left him little choice, but still, the reasoning goes – and this is probably perceived as the mark of true genius – he was able to transcend the situation to some extent, at least, and "mend" a few of the spectators' "hearts."

Seventy-three years later Maine wrote that Aristophanes' "indecency is due, partly to the survival at the festivals of Dionysus of very primitive forms of worship, and partly to the simple and outspoken frankness of the Greeks on topics which modern taste leaves rigorously unmentioned" (viii). This sort of statement tends to turn Aristophanes into some kind of "noble savage," and so to make him more acceptable to the receiving culture, not least by subtly confirming that culture's view of itself as superior to most, if not all others. Twenty-five years later, Way states that "this loose jesting was part of the tradition of the theatre. It had the sanction of immemorial prescription" (xix). Way's statement echoes Wheelwright's in part, but falls short of suggesting that Aristophanes actually did transcend his society.

Other translators try to merge the poetics of Aristophanes with a poetics acceptable in their own culture. Alan Sommerstein points out in his introduction that "some of the songs I have written with existing music in mind" (37). He goes on to define some of that music, designed to make the Attic comedy look more like a light operetta, as "well-known traditional tunes" (37), whereas other incidental music is taken from "the operas of Gilbert and Sullivan" (37). In one of the funniest scenes of the play, Kinesias, who has just been cheated out of sex by his wife Myrrhine, "bursts into a sorrowful song" (220). The song is addressed to his own "woeful" penis and "may be sung to 'The Blue Bells of Scotland' " (252). Similarly, Gilbert Seldes states in his introduction that

> The original play would have run some forty minutes and a great part of this would have been taken up by lengthy choruses for which our ears are no longer grateful, and by secondary scenes which had meanings for the Greeks twenty centuries ago, but have none for us. Some of the major scenes, however, have implications which Aristophanes had no need to work out and they have given the clue to the new scenes which have been added.
>
> (xi)

These new scenes have been added not only to make the play look more like what theater-goers of Seldes's own day and age had come to expect, but also to make an actual performance of it possible: since the very format of a theatrical performance has changed so much over the centuries, Aristophanes has to be made to fit the contemporary format. The alternative would be to leave him unperformed. Therefore, before one casts philological stones at Seldes, one could do worse than entertain the notion that he did not want to "disfigure" Aristophanes, but to actually "save" him for his own time. A classical philologist would think of Aristophanes' poetics as absolute; a man of the theater would not.

Seldes accordingly adds an introductory scene in which the chorus of old women explains to the audience what is going to happen, in the best tradition of the "well-made play." The same chorus actually dresses up the Athenian magistrate for a mock funeral as suggested (but not carried out) in the original text, puts him on a litter, and has him carried away by the chorus of old men, thus adding some – in Seldes's opinion no doubt much needed – action to the play. The scene between

Kinesias and Myrrhine is expanded to include similar games of advances and rejections between other soldiers and their wives, thus achieving a "choric" effect much closer to that usually seen in the musical than in Greek comedy, and one for which Seldes thinks "our ears" are likely to be more "grateful."

In the introduction to *Aikin Mata,* their rewriting (translation/adaptation? – the term rewriting absolves us of the necessity to draw borderlines between various forms of rewriting, such as "translation," "adaptation," "emulation") of *Lysistrata,* T. W. Harrison and J. Simmons state that "by restoring music and dance to an integral place in a production of Greek Comedy, the play itself could be performed in a manner nearer to the Greek than the kind of productions one has in European theatre" (9), hinting that the poetics of African theater are closer to those of Greek comedy than those of contemporary European theater. The unstated ideological assumption is, of course, that African culture is closer to what is generally considered the "cradle" of European civilization than contemporary Europe itself, even though Europe imposed its own culture on Africa in the name of "civilization." Harrison and Simmons mention specifically "masquerades like the Yoruba *Egungun* of Oshogbo with their dual sacred and profane functions as ancestor spirits and as comic entertainers" (10). Accordingly, in *Aikin Mata,* the chorus of old men and the chorus of old women actually fight to the accompaniment of drums. The Athenian magistrate is given the local title of "Alkali" and the old women "remove their shawls, tie them together, then run around Alkali, winding the cloth around him until he cannot move" (42). *Aikin Mata* also makes the struggle between matriarchy and patriarchy, which may well have been at the origin of *Lysistrata,* more explicit in the African context. The leader of the men's chorus addresses the women as "descendants of stern matriarchs" (36), and the two choruses sing praise songs for each other, interjecting another element taken from traditional African poetics. One of the songs sings the praises of Queen Amina of Zazzau, a warrior queen "beautiful and brave/Conquering as far as Kworarafa" (50). The rewriting of Aristophanes in this fashion seems to be designed to make him part and parcel of African culture, a "classic" in that culture in a way that is not within the power of the "Penguin Classics" rewritings used in African universities. Conversely, the "transposition" of classical Greek culture to Africa appears designed to suggest the existence of a common culture, and to raise questions about the legitimacy of claims made by one part of that "common culture" to superiority over the other part.

Ideology and poetics particularly shape the translator's strategy in solving problems raised by elements in the Universe of Discourse of the original and the linguistic expression of that original. The two problems coalesce in *Lysistrata* – as in other plays by Aristophanes – in the guise of the "cultural stereotype." Aristophanes introduces Dorians (Spartans and Megarans) on the Athenian stage, and the – to Athenians uncouth – way they speak Greek produces a comic effect. Perhaps the link between ideology on the one hand and strategies used for solving Universe-of-Discourse and linguistic problems on the other is nowhere as obvious as in the justifications used by translators to maintain in their translations some of the linguistic and cultural differentiations Aristophanes uses in the original. Lindsay states in a footnote that the translator has put the speech of the Spartan characters in Scotch dialect, which is related to English about as was the Spartan dialect to the speech of Athens. The Spartans, in their character, anticipated the shrewd, canny, uncouth Scotch highlander of modern times.

(26)

The Lindsay translation's popularity in Scotland may not have been overwhelming, especially not since a Scottish translator would, presumably, make the Spartans speak cockney. For similar reasons, Sutherland's translation may not go over too well in the south of the United States. His Dorians speak with a southern accent because Dorian "sounded rustic and yet could suggest aggressive pomposity, like certain Texan subvarieties of our Southern norm" (xiv). Neither translator stops to consider either the "validity" of the stereotypes, cultural-mechanisms to "affirm" the superiority of one subgroup over another, or the probable anachronistic effect of the use of "Scotch" or Texan in classical Athens.

Other nodes where ideology and/or poetics are seen to inspire strategies for dealing with problems related to Universe of Discourse, or simply discourse, are enumerated by Moses Hadas in his introduction to the Bantam Aristophanes: "allusions to contemporary persons, events or usages, special connotations of words" (2) – also implying *double entendre* – as well as "the volume of literary allusion which the audience was expected to recognize" (9). In his 1820 introduction, John Hookham Frere had already sketched the two mutually incompatible strategies available to translators grappling with these problems. With the benefit of hindsight we can link each of his archetypal translators to a certain ideology and a certain poetics. The first archetype is that of the "faithful translator," who

renders into English all the conversational phrases according to their grammatical and logical form, without any reference to the current usage which had affixed to them an arbitrary sense and appropriated them to a particular and definite purpose. He retains scrupulously all the local and personal peculiarities, and in the most rapid and transient allusions thinks it his duty to arrest the attention of the reader with a tedious explanatory note.

(xvi)

The archetypal translator just described tends to be conservative in both ideological and poetological terms. He translates the way he does out of reverence for the cultural prestige the original has acquired. The greater that prestige, the more "grammatical and logical" the translation is likely to be, especially in the case of texts regarded as the "foundation texts" of a certain type of society: the Bible, the Quran, *The Communist Manifesto*. This translator will use the "explanatory note" to ensure that the reader reads the translation – interprets the text, and certainly the foundation text – in the "right" way. He will also use the note to "resolve" any discrepancies that may be thought to exist between the actual text of the original and the current authoritative interpretation of that text, gladly changing both translation and notes as that interpretation changes.

Frere's "Spirited Translator,"

> on the contrary, employs the corresponding modern phrases; but he is apt to imagine that a peculiar liveliness and vivacity may be imparted to his performance by the employment of such phrases as are particularly connected with modern manners; and if at any time he feels more than usually anxious to avoid the appearance of pedantry, he thinks he cannot escape from it in any way more effectively than by adopting the language and jargon of the day. The peculiarities of ancient times he endeavors to represent by substituting in their place the peculiarities of his own time and nation.
>
> (xvii)

This archetypal translator is not conservative in either poetological or ideological terms. He is less awed than the "faithful translator" by the prestige of the original; indeed, it is often his intention to shock his audience by "updating" the original in such a way that it tends to lose at least some of its "classical" status. He gladly takes the risks involved in anachronism. His rewriting is, in essence, subversive, designed to make the reader question both the prestige of the original and its "received" interpretation in both poetological and ideological terms. Struggles between rival poetics are often sparked off by translations, and not seldom fought also by means of translations. Needless to say, this way of translating is not without risks where foundation texts are involved: many a "spirited" Bible translator, for instance, was burned at the stake, and the faithful were not allowed to translate the Quran.

It is easy to see which archetype William James Hickie chose for his model. Hickie states in his introduction that he "has endeavoured to give what Aristophanes actually wrote, as far as could be accomplished in English words, excepting in passages of extreme indelicacy, which are necessarily paraphrased" (v–vi). Paraphrase joins the "explanatory note" to ensure the "right" reading of the text. Douglass Parker, on the other hand, represents the contemporary avatar of the opposite archetype. He states in his introduction that he

> aims at recreating in American English verse what I conceive to have been Aristophanes' essential strategies in Greek. To do this, fields of metaphor have often been changed, jokes added in compensation for jokes lost, useless proper names . . . neglected.
>
> (4)

Whereas the conservative translator works on the level of the word or the sentence, the "spirited" translator works on the level of the culture as a whole, and of the functioning of the text in that culture. Yet, in the course of time, many translations succeed each other and sometimes they are diametrically opposed to each other.

One may well ask what relevance this fact – amply demonstrated here – may have for the vexed question of "fidelity" and "freedom" in translation. If we accept that translations get published, whether they are "faithful" or not, and that there is little one can do to prevent an "unfaithful" translation from projecting its own image of the original, that ought to be an end to the matter. "Faithfulness" is just one translational strategy that can be inspired by the collocation of a certain ideology with a certain poetics. To exalt it as the only strategy possible, or even allowable, is as utopian as it is futile. Translated texts as such can teach us much about the interaction of cultures and the manipulation of texts. These topics, in turn, may be of more interest to the world at large than our opinion as to whether a certain word has been "properly" translated or not. In fact, far from being "objective" or "value-free," as their advocates would have us believe, "faithful translations" are often inspired by a conservative ideology.

When the Boeotian delegate to the women's conference arrives, near the beginning of the play, Lysistrata exclaims: "Nē Di hos Boiotia/kalon g' echousa to pedion" [By Zeus, a Boeotian allright, she has a beautiful plain] (87). Calonice, Lysistrata's friend, remarks: "Kai nē Dia kompotata tēn blecho ge paratetilmene" [and by Zeus the pennyroyal has been plucked clean from it in the most elegant fashion] (88–9). The 1968 edition of Liddell and Scott dutifully translates the past participle *paratetilmenos* as "clean-plucked," and adds: "a practice among voluptuaries and women," suggesting that even such bastions of "objectivity" as dictionaries might have some kind of ideology behind them.

The anonymous translator of *Aristophanes. The Eleven Comedies* renders the dialogue as follows: "Ah! my pretty Boeotian friend, you are as blooming as a garden./Yes, on my word! And the garden is so prettily weeded too!" (232). He then proceeds to add an "explanatory note," though not necessarily a "tedious" one:

> the allusion, of course, is to the "garden of love," the female parts, which it was the custom with the Greek women, as it is with the ladies of the harem in Turkey to this day, to depilate scrupulously, with the idea of making themselves more attractive to men.
>
> (232)

The word "depilate" may have somewhat of a distancing effect, but the reader gets a pretty particular idea of what is going on.

Hickie turns the Bohn Classical Library translation, usually considered a monument of faithfulness, into "a Boeotian with a beautiful bosom/And, by Jove, with the hair very neatly plucked out" (393). It should be obvious that faithfulness in this translation has nothing to do with knowledge of Greek. Hickie knows very well what he is translating wrong and why he is doing it. No supernatural force has suddenly smitten him with amnesia or removed the relevant page from his dictionary. His ideology quite simply will not allow him to translate what is on the page. By submitting to the dictates of that ideology he makes nonsense of the original, except perhaps if we are willing to consider the somewhat remote possibility that Greek women did, indeed, have hair on their chests. But the woman in question is from Thebes, not Sparta, which would interfere with one of our cultural stereotypes. It should perhaps also be noted that, if one is to mention any part of the female anatomy at all within the confines of Hickie's ideology, the "bosom" has been rendered innocuous enough by cliché to assume an almost metonymic role, even though the metonymy would tend to stretch the imagination somewhat in this case.

Housman, whose ideology prescribes the exaltation of women on their way to liberation, accordingly renders the same dialogue as: "O fair Boeotia, with the full sweet breast/And locks wherein the sunlight seems to rest" (11). Not only does his Boeotian woman have hair; she also grows it in acceptable places. In other (rewritten) words: Greek suffragettes cannot be subjected to even faintly erotic *double entendre:* Parker, on the other hand, makes the *double entendre* more obvious by means of the judicious handling of stage directions:

Lysistrata:
As they inspect Ismenia
              Ah, picturesque Boiotia:
her verdant meadows, her fruited plain . . .
Kalonike:
Peering more closely
              Her sunken
garden where no grass grows. A cultivated country.
                                                          (13)

The disjunction between what is said and what is done on the stage renders the dialogue funny, presumably reproducing the intentions of Aristophanes.

Consider next an object and a concept that belonged to Aristophanes' Universe of Discourse. The object appears in line 109. "Ouk eidon," says Lysistrata, "oud olisbon oktodaktulon." She goes on to say: "hos en an hēmin skutine pikouria." Since the Milesians abandoned the Athenian cause, she complains, she has not seen "a single eight-fingered *olisbos* which could be a leather solace for us." An *olisbos,* Liddell and Scott obligingly inform us, is a "penis coriaceus." After briefly consulting the nearest Latin dictionary, we are able to find out that the phrase means: leather penis. The conservative translator would stop at this point; the "spirited" one might perhaps go on to something like "leather dildo." The Milesians were famous for manufacturing these items, and when they abandoned the Athenian cause the women of Athens were faced with a dire calamity indeed.

Housman omits the line altogether: suffragettes do not use this kind of thing. Hickie translates, but manages to do it in such a way that the reader still does not know what Lysistrata is talking about (he is definitely not trying to convey information). His translation reads: "I have not seen a thing of the kind which might have consoled us in the absence of our husbands" (394). He does supply a further "explanatory note" stating that "the Milesians, at the instigation of Alcibiades, had revolted in the Summer of the year 412" (394). It is well known that Athens lost one ally after another during the closing years of the Peloponnesian war, but the reader remains somewhat puzzled as to why the defection of the Milesians, in particular, is such a blow. Wheelwright also opts for the cryptic, for ideological reasons, perhaps confusing the reader as he does so. His translation reads: "For since we were betrayed by the Milesians/I have not seen a vase eight fingers long/ That we might have a leather consolation" (68). The reader may be excused for wondering about the strange Athenian custom of putting flowers in leather vases.

Fitts translates: "I've not seen so much, even/as one of those devices they call Widows' Delight" (10). Dickinson omits the lines altogether, and merely translates the preceding line: "Not even the ghost of a lover's/Been left to us women" (84). Harrison and Simmons quite logically translate: "there's little consolation in a *kwaroro*" (20), informing the reader in a footnote that a "kwaroro" is a "woven penis-sheath worn by the pagan tribes of the Plateau."

The concept belonging to Aristophanes' Universe of Discourse is that of Herakles' dinner. Towards the middle of the play Kinesias, the husband of one of the women who occupy the Acropolis, comes either to fetch her back home or, at least, to make her sleep with him. She leads him on, always "forgetting" something that is needed to make their marital duties more comfortable (a pillow, perfume), and she finally runs off just before he thinks he will be able to have sex with her. Kinesias voices his disappointment as follows: "all e to peos tod Hērakles ksenizetai" [but this penis here is waited on like Heracles] (line 928). The anonymous translator of the *Eleven Comedies* renders the line as follows: "Oh dear, oh dear! They treat my poor self for all the world like Herakles" (275). He adds in an "explanatory note":

> The comic poets delighted in introducing Heracles (Hercules) on the stage as an insatiable glutton, whom the other characters were forever tantalizing by promising toothsome dishes and then making him wait indefinitely for their arrival.
>
> (275)

The footnote makes the analogy clear to the reader, who can then really "understand" the line he or she just read in the text. The immediacy of understanding so important in comedy is, of course, totally lost. Being "faithful" to the original, Hickie again manages to translate something the reader, who is deprived of all "explanatory notes," will not be able really to understand: "Truly my carcase is entertained like Hercules" (429). Fitts does basically the same thing, fifty-two years later: "I don't suppose even Herakles/would stand for this" (81), rather easily deflating the *double entendre*.

Lindsay tries to incorporate the explanation of the concept into the concept as such: "They treat you just like Heracles at a feast/With cheats of dainties" (89). Sommerstein also opts for the "explanatory note" to supplement his rendering of the line as "This is a Heracles' supper and no mistake!" (219). Only Sutherland ("Poor prick, the service around here is terrible! [34]) and Parker ("What a love-feast! Only the table gets laid!" [66]) opt for rendering the basic information by eschewing the concept that served as its vehicle in the original. By doing so, they may arguably be said to remain much more "faithful" to that original than their colleagues who remain tied to the word and do not see the function of that word within the totality of the scene, or even the whole text.

Literary allusions represent another type of Universe of Discourse element. In their discussion with the magistrate, the women are making fun of the men strutting around Athens in full martial regalia and committing acts of valor like the following: "heteros d'au Thraks pelten seion kakontion hosper ho Tereus/ededitteto tēn ischadopolin kai tas orupepeos katepinen" [Another, like a Thracian, shaking a small light shield and a spear, like Tereus/frightened the dealer in figs and gobbled up the olives] (563–4). *Tereus* is the title of a lost play by Aristophanes' best enemy, Euripides. Sutherland gives us the author, but not the play: "and a Thracian who, brandishing shield and spear/like some savage Euripides staged once" (22). The anonymous translator of the *Eleven Comedies* gives us the play, but not the author: "There was a Thracian warrior too, who was brandishing his lance like Tereus in the play" (257). Rogers and Lindsay follow basically the same strategy, but most translators side with Housman and make no attempt at all to save the allusion, either because they give it up as a lost cause, or because they "compensate" for it at some other place in the play.

In lines 138–9, Lysistrata complains: "Ouk etos aph hēmon eisin hai tragodiai/ ouden gar esmen plēn Poseidon kai skaphē" (not for nothing are the tragedies about us/we are nothing but Poseidon and ship). The allusion, as Hickie tells us in an "explanatory note," is to "the Sophoclean tragedy of *Tyro,* where the beautiful girl appears with Neptune in the beginning, and at the close with two little boys, whom she exposes in a boat" (359–60). Housman changes the allusion in accordance with his ideology: "Oh, wretched race, which makes all Greece its grave!/ Women be vessels driven by wind and wave" (15) – but Greek suffragettes do not sleep with gods into the bargain. Wheelwright translates literally, but the allusion is lost on an audience that has not heard of *Tyro*: "The Tragedies describe us not in vain;/For we are nought save Neptune and his bark" (69). Rogers abandons the allusion as the cultural vehicle suited to the original and simply gives the information Aristophanes presumably intended to convey: "Always the same: nothing but loves and cradles" (165). Parker and Way try to steer a middle course, conveying the information intended in the original and linking it to Greek drama in general, not to the specific play Aristophanes had in mind. Parker writes: "We're perfect raw material for Tragedy,/the stuff of heroic lays. Go to bed with a god/and then get rid of the baby" (16). Way renders the same line as: "No wonder we are pilloried on the stage!/Act One with the usual 'God and the Girl' begins;/Act Two trots out the inevitable twins" (10).

On the whole, most translators do not try to convey the literary allusions, except in an "explanatory note." Maybe because allusions point to the final, real aporia of translation, the real untranslatable, which does not reside in syntactic transfers or semantic constructions, but rather in the peculiar way in which cultures all develop their own "shorthand," which is what allusions really are. A word or phrase can evoke a situation that is symbolic for an emotion or a state of affairs. The translator can render the word or phrase and the corresponding state of affairs without much trouble. The link between the two, which is so intricately bound up with the foreign culture itself, is much harder to translate.

It remains to say a few words about the final category in translation: language. The relative neglect with which language is treated here is, of course, intentional, but will be remedied to some extent in Chapter 7. For now, I simply want to make the point that, contrary to traditional opinion, translation is not primarily "about" language. Rather, language as the expression (and repository) of a culture is one element in the cultural transfer known as translation.

Toward the end of the play the following dialogue takes place between the Athenian magistrate and the Spartan emissary:

> All'estukas, o miarotate
> – Ou ton Di'ouk egonga; med au pladdie
> Ti d'esti soi todi?
> – Skutala Lakonika.
>
> (989–91)

Sutherland translates:

> But you have an erection, oh you reprobate!
> – Bah Zeus, Ah've no sech thing! And don't you fool around!
> And what have you got there?
> – A Spahtan scroll-stick, suh.
>
> (37)

Sommerstein gives us the Scottish/English variant on the American north/south theme:

> Why, you rascal, you've got prickitis!
> – No, I hanna. Dinna be stupid.
> Well, what's that, then?
> – It's a standard Spartan cipher-rod.
>
> (221)

Harrison and Simmons oblige with the Standard/Pidgin English variation on the same theme:

> But what is that thing?
> – Dey done give me powa to say
> (He looks down at his groin)
> Wetin? . . . Na Shango staff.
>
> (64)

A Shango staff is, of course, a staff used during the ritual worship of the god Shango. The point is made, however: it is very difficult to render connotations in translation, or different levels of diction, or, a priori, different dialects or idiolects.

Connotations and levels of diction also tend to belong to the "cultural shorthand" referred to above, as do proper names. Or, to put it in a more general way, whenever language moves on the illocutionary, rather than the locutionary level, the level of effect rather than that of communication, it threatens to become an aporia for translators. Dialects and idiolects tend to reveal the translators' ideological stance toward certain groups thought of as "inferior" or "ridiculous," both inside their culture and outside.

It might be said that comedy, as analyzed in this chapter, is a special case in translation because it highlights the ideological factor to such a great extent. But what if translation as a whole is a special case – a case in which the manipulation of texts can be most clearly documented, because the original and the manipulated text can be put side by side and analyzed comparatively? And what if all literature is, to some extent, transmitted of necessity in the same manipulatory manner?

5 Translation: ideology

On the construction of different Anne Franks

There are all kinds of statements in Anne Frank's diary that make it obvious that she wanted to be a writer and that she wanted her diary published after World War Two, long before Bolkestein, a minister in the Dutch cabinet in exile in London, broadcast a message to the occupied Netherlands over the BBC, urging his countrymen "to make a collection of diaries and letters after the war" (Paape 162). That collection was made, and it has since grown into the "Rijksinstituut voor Oorlogsdocumentatie," or State Institute for War Documentation, which published the most complete edition of the *Dagboeken van Anne Frank* (Anne Frank's diaries) forty-four years after the Bolkestein broadcast.

A comparison between the original, 1947 Dutch edition of the diary and the material collected in the 1986 edition gives us insight into the process of "construction" of an image of the writer, both by herself and by others. A further comparison between the Dutch original and the German translation sheds light on the "construction" of the image of a writer who belongs to one culture in – and especially for – another.

I shall quote only one of the many statements in the diary attesting Anne Frank's ambition to become a writer or, at least, a journalist: "I have other ideas as well, besides *Het Achterhuis*. But I will write more fully about them some other time, when they have taken a clearer form in my mind" (Mooyaart-Doubleday 194). This, at least, is in the English translation of the Dutch text as published in 1947. The corresponding entry (for May 11, 1944) in the original diaries, first published in the 1986 Dutch edition, also contains a detailed plot for a short story entitled "Cady's Life" and based on the life of Anne's father, Otto Frank (Paape 661). The short story had already "taken a clearer form" in Anne Frank's mind and was probably suppressed by Otto, or by Contact, the publisher of the 1947 Dutch edition.

When it became clear to Anne that the diary could, and should be published, she began to rewrite it. The original entries were made in notebooks; the rewritten version was produced on loose-leaf paper. Anne Frank was unable to finish the rewriting. Both the notebooks and the loose-leaf version were recovered by Miep, one of the Dutch employees of the Frank firm who helped the Franks and others to hide out in the *Achterhuis*. Miep discovered the material after the German Sicherheitsdienst had arrested the Franks and their friends, and taken them away (see Paape 69–88).

Anne Frank's own rewriting of the entries in the original diary amounts to a kind of "auto-editing." In editing herself she seems to have had two objectives in mind, one personal and the other literary. On the personal level, she disclaims earlier statements, especially about her mother, "Anne, is it really you who mentioned hate? Oh, Anne, how could you?" (Mooyaart-Doubleday 112), and about more intimate subjects: "I am really ashamed when I read those pages that deal with subjects I prefer to imagine more beautiful" (Paape 321). The entry for January 2, 1944, signals a turning away from the personal and toward the literary: "This diary is of great value to me, because it has become a book of memoirs in many places, but on a good many pages I could certainly put 'past and done with' " (Mooyaart-Doubleday 112). What is "past and done with" on the personal level becomes material for the literary rewrite.

An obvious example of "literary" editing is the description of one of Anne's encounters with Peter, the boy whose parents share the Franks' hiding place and who becomes Anne's first real love. The original entry reads: "as I sat almost in front of his feet" (Paape 504). The rewritten entry (for February 14, 1944) reads: "I . . . went and sat on a cushion on the floor, put my arms around my bent knees and looked at him attentively" (Mooyaart-Doubleday 132). The "edited" pose is much more in keeping with what Anne must have seen in the movie magazines she so avidly read. It is a very close approximation of the pose her culture expects the young heroine (in the theatre or film version of *The Life of Anne Frank,* for instance) to assume. It is a Universe-of-Discourse element (one might even say cliché) consciously inserted into the text.

An example of more consciously literary editing occurs in the entry for May 13, 1944. The original entry mentions a tree "stuck full of leaves" (Paape 662); the rewritten entry has the phrase, which amounts to a literary cliché in Dutch, "loaded down with leaves" (Paape 662). The most obvious example of literary editing is represented by the decision to change the names of all those who have, since January 2, 1944, become "characters" in a "story." Anne Frank obviously thought this a necessary strategy for the "book entitled *Het Achterhuis*" (she is most definitely not referring to it as a "diary") she "wanted to publish . . . after the war" (Mooyaart-Doubleday 194). Consequently, Anne Frank appears as "Anne Robin" in the loose-leaf version.

Anne Frank was not the only editor of Anne Frank's diary, however. When Otto Frank, her father, came back to Amsterdam after the war, he was given both the notebook and the loose-leaf versions of the diary. He produced a typescript of the material, in German, and sent it to his mother in Switzerland, who could not read Dutch. This typescript apparently vanished later on, but Otto Frank produced a second typescript which was to become the textual basis of the 1947 Dutch edition of the diary, and of the translations made into many languages since. A comparison between the original material now available in the 1986 *Dagboeken* and the 1947 Dutch edition merely shows that editing has taken place. It does not show who actually edited what over and beyond Anne Frank's own "auto-edits," which stop when the family was arrested and taken away.

Otto Frank tried to get his daughter's diary published after the war, both in the Netherlands and in Germany. He tried a few Dutch publishers and was eventually successful. Contact, one of the Dutch publishing houses, agreed to publish the typescript, but on condition that changes be made. Since Otto Frank had already made some changes of his own, and since Anne Frank had rewritten most of the original entries, the difference between the original material and the published version is like a palimpsest. It is pointless to speculate as to who changed what, but it is possible, and enlightening, to draw up a topology of the changes made. These can be said to belong to three categories: some changes are of a personal nature, some are ideological, and some belong in the sphere of patronage.

On the "personal" level, details of no possible importance to anyone are omitted. Also on that level, "unflattering" references to friends, acquaintances, or indeed members of the family are omitted as well. The description of all of Anne's classmates (Paape 207) has disappeared from the 1947 edition, as have references to her mother and "Mrs Van Daan." Anne tells her father that she loves him much more than she loves her mother (Paape 284), and Mrs Van Daan, whose real name, preserved in the first draft of the diary, was "Van Pels," is accused of greed (Paape 240) and overeating (Paape 282). Yet many unflattering references to both women remain in the 1947 edition, which leaves the reader a little puzzled as to the criteria for editing that were followed. There may well not have been any, except for the desire to protect people's reputations. This desire continues to manifest itself in the 1986 Dutch edition, which is still not complete.

On page 449 of the 1986 edition, for instance, we are told in a footnote that "Anne Frank gives a very unfriendly and partly inaccurate description of her parents' marriage in the 47 lines that have been omitted here. This passage has been deleted at the request of the Frank family." The personal obviously interferes with the literary. Or, if you wish, the editors decide to bend to one kind of ideological constraint.

Lines that may have been important for the (auto-)construction of the character "Anne Robin" have been omitted so as not to give the impression that the writer Anne Frank did not entirely correspond to the ideologically sanctioned image of what a fourteen-year-old should be – at the time she was (re)writing the diary. Similarly, unflattering references to the personal life of "M. K.," an acquaintance of the Franks who seems to have collaborated with the Germans and given promiscuously of her person, are omitted: "24 words have been deleted at the request of the person in question" (Paape 647). Moreover, as we are informed on the same page, the initials M. K. were chosen at random because the person did not want her own initials used.

References to bodily functions of all kinds have also been omitted, as has a rather graphic description of a case of hemorrhoids (Paape 282). Like many persons her age, Anne Frank appears to have been more than somewhat interested in bodily functions, especially defecation, because defecation was for a while associated in her mind with the birth of children, witness the description of defecation in a children's book called *Eva's jeugd,* which she quotes at some length (Paape 285).

In the original version of the diary, Anne Frank keeps addressing (imaginary) letters to various friends left behind in the "real" world for a few weeks after the Frank family went into hiding. The letters are "imaginary" in that they were written, but could never be sent. These letters represent a marked deviation from the original intention of the diary as Anne Frank herself conceived it. Originally the diary was to take the place of the "really good girl friend" Anne Frank never had. This is also the reason why (nearly) all entries in the diary were written in the form of letters and addressed to "Kitty," the name Anne Frank had given her diary/imaginary friend. The letters that have been omitted suggest that Kitty was not enough, at least not initially, and that Anne Frank/Robin found it much more difficult to adapt to the sudden cataclysmic change in her life than is implied by the 1947 edition. In these letters she continues to act as if communication between herself and the real friends she had left behind in the world outside is still possible, much as it was before the Franks went into hiding. She even writes a friend called "Conny" that "you are welcome to stay with me for a while" (Paape 267). Fantasies about life after the war (Paape 301) and, especially, a trip to Switzerland with her father, which point in the same "escapist" direction, have also been omitted from the Dutch 1947 edition.

The topic of sex acts as a link between the "personal" and the "ideological" edits. Meulenhoff, the first Dutch publisher to evaluate the manuscript of Anne Frank's diary for publication, refused to publish it because of "the very personal nature of the diary and the sexual musings it contains" (Paape 78). Similarly, De Neve, an editor at Contact, told Otto Frank that "spiritual advisers objected to the printing of certain passages (about masturbation, for instance)" (Paape 80). As may be expected, the "sexual musings" referred to are mainly concerned with Anne Frank's own awakening sexuality. They consist of a description of a discharge in her underwear preceding the onset of menstruation (Paape 286), of menstruation itself (Paape 304, 598), of her genitals (Paape 294, 583–4), of different strategies used to find out about sex without having to ask grown-ups (Paape 562, 576) – of all the elements, in short, that would fit the "heroine" of any "Life of Anne Frank" published from the sixties onwards, but not the heroine of the diary published in 1947.

It is of course also possible that the person Anne Frank may indeed have been "really ashamed" when she (re-)"read those pages" (Paape 321), and that she herself may have omitted them in the loose-leaf version. They have been omitted in any case, as has Bep/Elli's story about an unwed mother (Paape 305) and the "dirty words" like "bordeel" (brothel) and "cocotte" Anne picked up from her reading (Paape 305). Finally, in the original diary Pfeffer (whose name is changed to "Dussel" in the loose-leaf version) "lives together with a Gentile woman, much younger than he is, and nice, and he is probably not married to her" (Paape 320). In the first published version of the diary, Dussel's wife "was fortunate enough to be out of the country when war broke out" (Mooyaart-Doubleday 51).

Another edit involving both the personal and the ideological concerns the Goldsmith/Goudsmit affair. Goldsmith was a lodger in the Franks' house in Amsterdam. After the Frank family went into hiding, they left him more or less in charge of their possessions. In the passages that have been omitted from the 1947 edition (Paape 256, 309), Anne Frank hints heavily at the probability that Goldsmith sold or otherwise disposed of the Frank possessions to his own advantage. These passages may have been omitted out of an unwillingness on the part of the Frank family to admit that they had been deceived, or out of a sense of solidarity, even piety, among the victims of the Holocaust.

The most obviously ideological omissions are those of the passages Anne Frank wrote on the problem of the emancipation of women. The longest passage, introduced by the question "Why woman occupies a position so much lower than man's among the nations" (Paape 692), is deleted in its entirety, and further passing references to the topic are either weakened or deleted.

Finally, it is obvious that Otto Frank bowed to constraints in the sphere of patronage, and it is also obvious that he had no other choice. The typescript of Anne Frank's diary had to conform to the specifications laid down by Contact, the publishing house, for its "Proloog" series, of which the diary would be a part. As a result, Contact's editor(s?) "Proposed 26 deletions, 18 of which were indeed carried out in the typescript" (Paape 82).

Anne Frank (perhaps the time has come to call her "Anne Frank") is subjected to further transformations in the German translation of her diary. That translation, based on Otto Frank's (second) typescript, was made early on by Anneliese Schütz, a friend of the Frank family. Anneliese Schütz was a journalist who had emigrated to the Netherlands to escape from the Nazis, just as the Franks had. Since Otto Frank was trying to publish the composite material labeled with his daughter's name, either in the Netherlands or in Germany, it stood to reason that he would allow a friend to translate his typescript into German, so that it could be offered to publishers in Germany. Anneliese Schütz translated from a typescript that had not yet been edited by the Contact editor(s), which is why the German translation contains references to sexuality which had been removed from the Dutch 1947 edition, and which were later inserted back into the English translation.

The "notorious" passage in which "Anne Frank" asks a girl friend (identified by name in the original entry) "whether, as proof of our friendship, we should feel one another's breasts" (Mooyaart-Doubleday 114) therefore appears in both the German and the English translations, but not in the Dutch 1947 original, nor in the French translation, which is entirely based on that original.

Otto Frank's evaluation of Anneliese Schütz's translation is, unfortunately, accurate. He states that she was "too old to do it, many expressions are schoolmarmish and not in the tone of youth. She has also misunderstood many Dutch expressions" (Paape 84). Among the most obvious are: "ogenschijnlijk" (Paape 201) [seemingly], which is translated as "eigentlich" [really] (Schütz 10); "daar zit hem de knoop" [something like "there's the rub," literally, "there sits the knot"] (Paape 201) becomes "ich bin wie zugeknöpft [I feel as if I'm buttoned up] (Schütz 10). "Zulke uilen" [such idiots] (Paape 215) is turned into "solche Faulpelze" [such lazy people] (Schütz 12); "Ongerust" [worried] (Paape 307) becomes "unruhig" [restless] (Schütz 39).

"Rot" [rotten] (Paape 372) is rendered by "rötlich" [reddish] (Schütz 64), a typical elementary classroom howler. "Rataplan" [the whole kit and caboodle] (Paape 402) becomes "Rattennest" [rat's nest] (Schütz 78). "Ik zat op springen" [I was about to explode] (Paape 529) is turned into "Ich wäre ihr am liebsten ins Gesicht gesprungen" [I would have loved to have jumped into her face] (Schütz 90). *Springen* can mean both "explode" and "jump" in Dutch, as it can in German too. Schütz opted for the homonym that does not fit the context. "Wat los en vastzit" [what is loose and what is secured] (Paape 595) turns into "Was nicht niet-und nagelfest ist" [what is not secured and fastened down] (Schütz 147), and "de landen die aan Duitsland grenzen" [the countries bordering on Germany – "grenzen" is a verb] (Paape 669) becomes "die an Deutschlands Grenzen" [those at Germany's borders – "Grenzen" is a plural noun] (Schütz 180).

As if more proof were needed, the Schütz translation once again illustrates the fact that publishers rarely care overmuch about the quality of the translation of any manuscript that either might not sell (as the Lambert Schneider Verlag, which published the *Tagebuch* in hardcover in 1950, may have thought) or sells very well (as the same publisher and, especially, the Fischer Verlag, which published the first paperback edition, must have thought after 1955). The fact that the Schütz translation was and is reprinted time and again also points to another institutional constraint: the pernicious influence of copyright laws which, in this case, even embarrasses the publisher. The most recent editions of the *Tagebuch* contain a note in which the publisher apologizes in veiled terms for the inferior quality of the translation and promises to issue a better translation as soon as legally possible.

The most famous of Schütz's "mistranslations" is that of the Dutch "er bestaat geen groter vijandschap op de wereld dan tussen Duitsers en Joden" [there is no greater enmity in the world than between Germans and Jews] (Paape 292), which is translated as: "eine grössere Feindschaft als zwischen *diesen* Deutschen und den Juden gibt es nicht auf der Welt!" [there is no greater enmity in the world than between *these* Germans and the Jews] (Schütz 37). The editors of the 1986 Dutch edition comment: "Otto Frank discussed this sentence with Anneliese Schütz and they came to the conclusion that '*diesen* Deutschen' corresponded more closely to what Anne had wanted to say" (Paape 85). This "mistranslation" is only one among many that have been made for reasons best described as ideological – a mixture of a more old-fashioned "ideology" based on a certain view of the world, and the more contemporary "ideology" of profit pure and simple. In Anneliese Schütz's own words: "a book you want to sell well in Germany . . . should not contain any insults directed at Germans" (Paape 86).

Schütz translates accordingly and tones down all instances of descriptions of Germans in Anne Frank's diary that could be construed as "insulting." As a result, the plight of the Jews in the Netherlands is, correspondingly, made to appear less harsh than it actually was. "Jodenwet volgde op Jodenwet" [one Jewish law followed the other] (Paape 203) is turned into "ein diktatorisches Gesetz folgte dem anderen" [one dictatorial law followed another] (Schütz 11), as if these laws had little or nothing to do with the Jews. The details of these laws, the terminology they were expressed in, are also hushed up. Where Anne Frank says her family had to leave Germany because they were "volbloed Joden" [full-blooded Jews] (Paape 202), Schütz translates simply: "Als Juden" [as Jews] (10).

When Otto Frank has given his wife's bicycle "bij Christenmensen in bewaring" [to Gentiles for safekeeping] (Paape 218), Schütz simply writes: "bei Bekannten" [to acquaintances] (14), thus obscuring the very distinct boundaries the Nazis wanted to draw between Jews and Gentiles all over Europe. When Mrs Van Daan "keerde terug en begon te kijven, hard, Duits, gemeen en onbeschaafd" [came back and began to scold, harsh, German, mean and uncivilized] (Paape 274), "German," used here as an adjective to convey a further insult, is left out in Schütz (34).

Anne Frank's description (based on hearsay) of Westerbork, the German concentration camp in the Netherlands from where Jews were shipped "East," as the current euphemism would have it, is weakened in a similar way. Anne Frank writes: "voor honderden mensen 1 wasruimte en er zijn veel te weinig WC's. De slaapplaatsen zijn alle door elkaar gegooid" [1 washroom for hundreds of people, and there are far too few toilets. The sleeping spaces have all been thrown together] (Paape 290). Schütz has: "viel zu wenig Waschgelegenheiten und WC's vorhanden. Es wird erzählt, dass in den Baracken alles durcheinander schläft" [far too few washing facilities and toilets available. It is said that they all sleep together in the barracks] (36–7). The translation suggests that there are more washrooms than just the one of the original, and the impact of the "sleeping together" in a disorderly fashion is weakened by the addition of "it is said."

The rest of the description, concerning the consequences of the state of affairs just mentioned, is simply omitted in the translation. Anne Frank writes on: "men hoort daardoor van verregaande zedeloosheid, vele vrouwen en meisjes, die er wat langer verblijf houden, zijn in verwachting" [therefore you hear of far-reaching immorality; many women and girls who stay there for a longer period of time are pregnant] (Paape 290). If this fact is not mentioned in the translation, the Germans, whose families and descendants are supposed to read the *Tagebuch,* also, quite logically, did not gas any pregnant women or girls in Auschwitz.

In the diary, Anne Frank is very upset by the German policy of shooting hostages, which she describes as follows: "zet de Gestapo doodgewoon een stuk of 5 gijzelaars tegen de muur" [the Gestapo simply puts 5 hostages or so against the wall] (Paape 292). The translation weakens this to "dann hat man einen Grund, eine Anzahl dieser Geiseln zu erschiessen" [they then have a reason to shoot a number of these hostages] (Schütz 37). "[T]hey" instead of the dreaded "Gestapo" makes the description seem somewhat less terrible, and "shoot" instead of "puts against the wall" "elevates" the act to a more abstract level.

Similarly, the person who might discover the secret entrance to the place where Anne and her family are hiding, grows in Anne's imagination into "een reus en hij was zo'n fascist als er geen ergere bestaat" [a giant, and he was such a fascist, no worse exists] (Paape 298). In German, the person has simply become "einen unüberwindlichen Riesen" [an unconquerable giant] (Schütz 39). The "fascist" has disappeared from the German text so as not to depress its sales. An analogous omission occurs in the translation of Anne Frank's statement on the languages spoken in the hideout: "toegestaan zijn alle cultuurtalen, dus geen Duits" [all civilized languages are allowed, so no German] (Paape 330). The German translation reads: "alle Kultursprachen, aber leise" [all civilized languages, but softly] (Schütz 46).

Anneliese Schütz uses omission to further political (and economic) advantage. Where Anne Frank writes: "de moffen niet ter ore komen" [not come to the ears of the Krauts] (Paape 490), the German translation reads: "den 'Moffen' nicht zu Ohren kommen" [not to come to the ears of the "Moffen"] (Schütz 114). A footnote explains "Moffen" as a "Spottname für die Deutschen" [abusive name for the Germans] (Schütz 114). "Mof," plural "Moffen," was indeed the wartime "abusive name" for the Germans. In the Dutch text, therefore, "Moffen" has quite an impact on the reader. That impact is undercut in German simply by the non-translation of the term. To a German reader, "Moffen" tends to sound "exotic," even when supplemented by a footnote, and not really insulting.

Not coincidentally the mean, aggressive cat in the warehouse is called "Moffi" by the inhabitants of the hideout. German readers, who either do not know what a "Mof" is until they reach page 114, and/or think of "Mof" as exotic after they have been enlightened, are likely to miss the point of the insult. Logically, the "Moffen" live in "Moffrika" (Paape 695), which Schütz leaves untranslated. It becomes "Bocheland" in English (Mooyaart-Doubleday 210) and "les Boches" in French (Caren and Lombard 269). The cat duly becomes "Bochi" in French (Caren and Lombard 91) and "Boche" in English (Mooyaart-Doubleday 68).

The English translation sometimes tries to convey the fact that the Franks and the others in hiding with them, all being German refugees, did not really speak standard Dutch but rather a mixture of Dutch and German, more Dutch than German in the case of the children, more German than Dutch where the parents are concerned. This mixture of languages helps to highlight the fact that the "characters" in the diary are people who have already been uprooted once and are now hiding from their former countrymen in mortal fear of their lives. None of this is conveyed by the German translation. Dussel, for instance, says in the original: "*Du kannst dies* toch van mij aannemen. Het kan mij natuurlijk niets schelen, *aber Du musst* het zelf weten" [(German italicized) *You can* take *this* from me. It does not matter to me, of course, *but you must* know for yourself] (Paape 412). Mooyaart-Doubleday, the English translator, tries: "But *du kannst* take this from me. Naturally I don't care a bit, *aber du* must know for yourself" (94).

Neither the German nor the French translator makes any attempt at all to render the mixture of languages. In fact, Schütz scales the heights of absurdity by "translating" Dussel's next "macaronic" statement, "ich mach das schon" [I'll take care of it] (Paape 502) as "Ich weiss schon was ich tue" [I know what I'm doing] (118).

Yet political, or politico-economic features are responsible for one set of changes only. There is another set of changes in the German text, also caused by ideological motivations, but of a less obvious, more insidious nature. Schütz consciously or unconsciously turns Anne Frank into the cultural stereotype of the "proper" young adolescent girl of a time that had not yet invented the teenager, "properly educated" as befits her social status, presumably to make her more acceptable to a fifties audience.

First, Schütz "cleans up" Anne Frank's language. Her friend Harry, for instance, will not be allowed to say in German what he says in Dutch. Whereas the Dutch Harry says: "Het is daar ook zo'n rommelzootje" [it's such a mess there] (Paape 221), the German Harry "echoes": "gefiel es mir da nicht" [I did not like it there] (Schütz 15). People who complain about their defecation ("ontlasting" [Paape 269]) in Dutch complain about their digestion ("Verdauung" [Schütz 32]) in German.

After a bombing raid on Amsterdam, Anne Frank writes that it will take days before all the victims have been dug up ("opgegraven" [Paape 389]). In German, the victims are "geborgen" [recovered] (Schütz 72) in a much more decorous way, which also takes the sting out of the horror. The chamber pot Anne Frank takes with her to the bathroom in the Dutch original (Paape 339) vanishes in German. It remains quite sensibly "pot de nuit" in French (Caren and Lombard 116) and becomes "pottie" in English (Mooyaart-Doubleday 88). When Dussel begins "vrouwen-verlangens te krijgen" in Dutch [get a desire for women] (Paape 679), he gets much more decorous "Frühlingsgefühle" [Spring feelings] (Schütz 184) in German. The German translation also completely leaves out Anne Frank's rather elaborate description of the way Mouschi, Peter's cat, urinates in the attic.

Second, Anne Frank has to behave "properly" for a child her age. She has to conform to what is considered proper cultural behavior for the upper-middle-class fourteen-year-old, even if that kind of "proper behavior" has been made less than a little ridiculous by the war and the living conditions in the hideout. When the Dutch Anne Frank is allowed to "lachen tot ik er buikpijn van krijg" [laugh until I get a bellyache] (Paape 446), the German Anne Frank is only allowed to do what German children do when they laugh, at least according to Anneliese Schütz: "unbeschwert und glücklich lachen" [laugh without a care and happily] (98).

The Dutch Anne Frank successfully accomplishes the following task: "uit een lichtblauwe onderjurk met kant van Mansa heb ik een hypermoderne dansjurk vervaardigd" [from one of Mansa's (mother's) light-blue slips with lace I made a hypermodern dancing dress] (Paape 469). The German Anne Frank has her mother do the same thing for her: "aus einem hellblauen Spitzenkleid hat Mansa mir ein hypermodernes Tanzkleid gemacht" [Mansa made me a hypermodern dance dress from a light-blue slip with lace of hers] (Schütz 107).

There are other things a young girl, German or not, of Anne Frank's age and social status is not supposed to know or do. When Anne Frank describes the flowers she gets for her birthday as "de kinderen van Flora" [the children of Flora] (Paape 198), thereby displaying her knowledge of mythology, which is one of her hobbies, Schütz will have none of this precocious name-dropping; in German, Anne Frank gets "Blumengrüsse" [flower greetings] (Schütz 19).

No effort is made to reproduce in German any of the stylistic effects Anne Frank tries to achieve in Dutch, as she does in the following example by means of the repetition of the word "koud" (cold). In Dutch, children walk "van hun koude woning weg naar de koude straat en komen op school in een nog koudere klas" [from their cold home to the cold street to end up in an even colder classroom at school] (Paape 349). In German, the children walk "aus der kalten Wohnung auf die nasse, windige Strasse und kommen in die Schule, in eine feuchte, ungeheizte

Klasse" [from their cold home to the wet, windy street and they arrive at school in a damp, unheated classroom] (Schütz 54).

Fourteen-year-old girls are also not allowed to sit in judgment on their mothers or elder sisters. Anne Frank writes in Dutch that she would never be satisfied with "zo'n bekrompen leventje" [such a limited life] (Paape 650) as her mother and Margot, her elder sister, seem willing to settle for. The German Anne Frank, on the other hand, writes "so ein einfaches Leben" [such a simple life] (Schütz 172). Finally, with a relentless logic that borders on the grotesque and should, properly speaking, render the whole of Anne Frank's endeavor useless or, at best, superfluous, the girls Anneliese Schütz models her Anne Frank on are not even supposed to keep diaries. Anne Frank writes in Dutch that there are certain things she does not intend "aan iemand anders mee te delen dan aan mijn dagboek, en een enkele keer aan Margot" [to communicate to anyone else but my diary, and once in a while to Margot] (Paape 705). In German, Anne Frank writes that she has things she is determined to "niemals jemandem mitzuteilen, höchstens einmal Margot" [never communicate to anyone, at the most once in a while to Margot] (Schütz 196). The diary, the object of the exercise, the text read all over the world, simply vanishes from the translation, sacrificed to the "image" of Anne Frank the German translator wishes to project.

"Proper" girls also write in a "proper" style. Creativity is actively discouraged in the German translation. When Anne Frank writes, "we zijn zo stil als babymuisjes" [we are as quiet as baby mice] (Paape 279), the German translation reads "wir verhalten uns sehr ruhig" [we are very quiet] (Schütz 35). When a bag of beans suspended against the door of the attic bursts, spilling its contents and leaving Anne standing "als een eilandje tussen de bonengolven" [like a small island among waves of beans] (Paape 318), the translation simply describes her as "berieselt von braunen Bohnen" [bedrizzled by brown beans] (Schütz 43).

When the Jews are led to "onzindelijke slachtplaatsen" [dirty slaughterhouses] (Paape 368), the "dirty" obviously has to disappear from the German translation, in which the Jews are simply "zur Schlachtbank geführt" [led to the slaughter bench] (Schütz 62). Finally, when the inhabitants of the hideout "kijken met bange voorgevoelens tegen het grote rotsblok, dat winter heet, op" [look up at the big rock called Winter with fearful apprehension] (Paape 422), they simply "sehen mit grosser Sorge dem Winter entgegen" [look ahead at winter with great worry] (Schütz 90).

The girl Anne Frank writing her diary has become the author Anne Frank because she herself and others were constrained by ideological, poetological, and patronage considerations. Once Anne Frank took the decision to rewrite for publication what Anne Frank had written, the person Anne Frank split up into a person and an author, and the author began to rewrite in a more literary manner what the person had written. Others responded to the constraints of ideology and patronage in her stead, and they did so as they saw fit. She had no say in the matter. That is why part of her experience, very definitely a formative part, is missing from the 1947 Dutch text, and why she has been made to conform, in German, to a cultural stereotype and made to water down the description of the very atrocities which destroyed her as a person.

6 Translation: poetics

The case of the missing *qasidah*

Of all the great literatures of the world, the literature produced in the Islamic system is arguably the least available to readers in Europe and the Americas. Any reader walking into a decent bookstore is likely to find anthologies of Chinese and Japanese literature, as well as fairly recent translations of important works, some even in cheap paperback editions. While there seems to be no comprehensive anthology of Indian literature, particularly not the literature produced in Dravidian languages, the classics of that literature are also available to a much greater extent than those of Islamic literature. In contrast, James Kritzeck's authoritative *Anthology of Islamic Literature,* originally published in hardback in 1964, at a price that militated against its wide dissemination among non-professional readers of Islamic, or any other literature, was made available in paperback only in 1975, and has not been reprinted since. Since Kritzeck worked with existing translations, some of which had been made by scholars for scholars and some by Victorian translators for the non-professional readers of their time, the contemporary reader may also be forgiven for not having experienced an aesthetic revelation when perusing the *Anthology.* As Kritzeck points out: "In recent years a considerable number of masterpieces of Islamic literature have individually displayed their merits through translation into Western languages" (3), but most of these translations have not been able to move the Western reader much more than many of those contained in Kritzeck's own anthology, with the result that "[F]ew of them have become widely known" (3).

Genres from non-European literatures have established themselves within European poetics. The *haiku* is now practiced all over the world. A genre belonging to the Islamic system also established itself within European poetics and enjoyed considerable popularity for a number of decades, significantly in the wake of a famous rewriting that could hardly be called a translation in the sense in which that word was used by the rewriter's contemporaries. Edward Fitzgerald's *Rubayat of Omar Khayyam,* published in 1859, introduced the *roba'i,* or quatrain into European poetics, and until about 1920 many poets of note in the literatures of Europe and the Americas tried their hand at the genre. In his anthology published in 1900, therefore, Epiphanius Wilson could write that some of these "little songs" might have "been written by 'Anacreon' Moore, and others by Catullus" (49). The quatrain's popularity has been waning since the 1920s, however, and shows few signs of reviving.

Furthermore, "Islamic peoples regard the *Rubayat* [and, one might add, the *Thousand and One Nights*] as quite inferior morsels of what their rich literatures contain" (Kritzeck 3). On the other hand, the *qasidahs*, "regarded as the supreme canon and model of poetic excellence" (Kritzeck 52) by readers, professional or not, inside the Islamic system, are hardly available in easily accessible translations in Europe and the Americas, either separately or as a group. The term *qasidah,* which has been used for about fifteen hundred years to designate these works, does not rate mention in the *Micropedia* of the current *Encyclopedia Britannica,* the compendium of what Western culture considers important. The sonnet, which has been practiced for a little more than half that time, rates a fairly extensive entry. The *Britannica's Macropedia* does mention the *qasidah* in the entry dedicated to the "Arts of the Islamic Peoples," but unaccountably neglects to mention the author of the *qasidah* I shall be concentrating on in this chapter: Labid Ibn Rakiah. The effect of this oversight would be comparable to the sudden omission of Swinburne, Tennyson, or Browning from entries devoted to Victorian English poetry or English poetry in general in major reference works of the Arabic world.

It is my contention that the reason for this sad state of affairs need not be sought among the writers of the *qasidahs,* but among those who have tried to rewrite them in terms acceptable within European and, later, Euro-American poetics. Indeed, as I hope to show in what follows, the reason, the fault, or both do not lie with the rewriters either, but rather with the incompatibility of the poetics of the European and the Islamic systems. The apparent failure to "naturalize" the *qasidah* in the Euro-American system to the degree that the *haiku,* for instance, or even the *roba'i* have been naturalized, has absolutely nothing to do with the competence of the rewriters: their knowledge of Arabic is not questioned. Simply, no rewriter has, as yet, found a "slot" in Euro-American poetics to fit the *qasidah.*

Nor is the incompatibility of the two poetics the only reason for the failure to naturalize the *qasidah.* That incompatibility is compounded by the relatively low prestige of Islamic culture in Europe and the Americas. This relatively low prestige, in turn, calls forth two reactions. The most radical reaction consists of a refusal to get to know Islamic culture. The second reaction consists of a willingness to make the acquaintance of Islamic literature, but strictly on the basis of a dominant/dominated relationship. Euro-American literature is seen as the "true" literature, and whatever Islamic literature has to offer is measured against that yardstick. This attitude in turn allows for a rather cavalier treatment of Islamic culture by those – other than professional scholars – who profess an interest in it. What Fitzgerald wrote to his friend E. B. Cowell on the subject of the Persian poets he was dealing with could without much exaggeration be extended to represent a not unwidely disseminated attitude toward Islamic literature as a whole: "It is an amusement for me to take what Liberties I like with these Persians who (as I think) are not Poets enough to frighten one from such excursions, and who really do want a little Art to shape them" (6: xvi). Fitzgerald, it is safe to say, would never have dared to take such "Liberties" with classical Greek or

Latin literature, because of the prestige enjoyed by these literatures in his time and since – at least in terms of designing syllabuses. Not only would there have been far too many scholars who could have corrected him, but Greek and Latin literature were (are?) considered the very foundations of the literature Fitzgerald was becoming a part of. He would have been undermining his own cultural base had he tried to take any "Liberties" with them. Persian and, by extension, Islamic literature were and are seen as marginal, "exotic," and can be treated with much less reverence.

Euro-American rewriters of Islamic literature seem to have approached their task either with a basic attitude of apology for what they were about to do, and that apology did, occasionally, modulate into barely disguised indifference, or even veiled contempt, or with a basic attitude of admiration which often made them look in their native or adopted literatures for analogies to those elements of the poetics of the Islamic system they tried to introduce into their own literatures.

In terms of ideology the two poles can be found quite early on in the process of the reception of Arabic literature into English. Apology dominates the introduction to Clément Huart's *History of Arabic Literature,* originally written in French, to be sure, but a shaper of Anglo-American attitudes toward Islamic literature in its English translation. Huart writes: "One burst of enthusiasm – it was but a flash – sent forth these men . . . to conquer the whole world. But the Bedouin fell back ere long into his primitive way of life" (2). The Arabs living in towns, on the other hand, were subject to "those vices which are the virtues of the primitive man – cunning, greed, suspicion, cruelty" (2). Indeed, they have hardly changed over fourteen centuries, since Huart goes on to say that those same vices "reign unchecked, even to this day, in the hearts of the dwellers in these inaccessible towns" (Huart 2).

Sir William Jones takes up the opposite position, but not without betraying a certain ignorance about the actual nature of the object of his admiration, when he writes:

> we must conclude that the Arabians, being properly conversant with the most beautiful objects, spending a calm and agreeable life in a fine climate, being extremely addicted to the softer passions, and having the advantage of a language singularly adapted to poetry, must be naturally excellent poets.
>
> (10: 340)

His panegyric is surpassed only by that of F. E. Johnson, an early translator of the *qasidahs,* who characterizes the pre-Islamic Arabs as:

> this nation, which was destined by God to rise to great importance later on, and to succeed the Romans in presiding over the destinies of a great part of the world . . . deserves all praise for the high state of culture, civilization and advancement which its people attained by means of self-development of those superior literary faculties with which it had pleased God to endow them.
>
> (vi)

W. S. Blunt, another admirer of early Islamic literature, puts the analogy strategy to use in the introduction to his translations of the *qasidahs*:

> in Europe the nearest analogy to it is perhaps to be found in the pre-Christian verse of Celtic Ireland, which by a strange accident was its close contemporary, and lost its wild natural impulse through the very same circumstance of the conversion of its pagan bards to an overmastering theology.
>
> (ix)

The point I am trying to make can be made quite independently of the validity of Blunt's analogy, or lack thereof. What I am trying to show is that Blunt and others felt the need to rewrite (pre-)Islamic literature in terms of a system their potential audience would be able to understand.

The analogy strategy can also be put to use in negative terms. If one is convinced that Western literatures constitute the "right" literature, one can also project that conviction back in time and pretend that only those literatures whose evolution is similar to that of Western literatures are worthy of comparison with Western literatures. Any literature whose history does not begin with anything comparable to the Homeric epics is, therefore, of necessity suspect. As Huart puts it: "That wondrous appanage of the Indo-European races, their power of translating historic or legendary events into mighty poems . . . has no existence in the brain of the peoples speaking the Semitic tongues" (5). These people, it is strongly implied, therefore do not just produce inferior literature; they also belong to an inferior race. Carlyle remarks in the same vein, but without drawing any racist consequences: "As no examples taken from any Epic or Dramatic poems, are found amongst the specimens here selected, it may be supposed that the Arabians were unacquainted with the two most noble exertions of the poet's art" (xi). He adds, however, that this is true only if we submit to a strict interpretation of Aristotle's poetics, which specifies that the epic has to be written in verse. A century or so later Nicholson is willing to relax this strict interpretation of Aristotle, though not completely. He observes that the longest of the *qasidahs* "is considerably shorter than Gray's *Elegy*" and goes on to state that "an Arabian Homer or Chaucer must have condescended to prose" (77).

Blunt also points out in his introduction that "moral blemishes not a few there are in all the poems, but one would not wish them absent, for they serve to point out the reality of the life described" (xvi). In Labid Ibn Rakiah's *qasidah* one of those blemishes might be the lot of the girl who plucks the lute. Polk's translation reads:

> With many a morning, limpid (draught and) the plucking of the singing girl
> On a lute as her thumb adjusts the string
> I hasten to satisfy the need of her while the cock crows at first light
> In order that I might drink a second round while the night's sleepers rouse themselves.
>
> (121–3)

Johnson obviously tries to shift the "blemish" from one "moral" category to another deemed more acceptable. He translates: "I hastened in the early morning before the crowing of the cock, to relieve my want for it (i.e. wine) that I might take a second draught from it, when the sleepers awoke" (115). Sixty-five years later, Arberry also opts for this solution, albeit by means of a use of language that might be considered somewhat unfortunate: "and a charming girl plucking/with nimble fingers the strings of her melodious lute;/yes, I've raced the cock bright and early, to get me my spirit's need/and to have my second wetting by the time the sleepers stirred" (146).

Blunt applies the same strategy, making use of the "archaic craftsmanship" propagated by Browning in the translation of older literature, which was supposed to result in diction of a timeless quality. Blunt perhaps also counted on this "time-less diction" to deflect attention from the fact that the writers of the *qasidahs,* and the characters they introduce see absolutely nothing wrong with what are "moral blemishes" to the Westerner. On the contrary: "All with them is frankly, inspirit-ingly, stupendously hedonistic" (Blunt xi). Not surprisingly, Blunt, who translated the *qasidahs* together with Lady Anne Blunt, had the translations privately pub-lished in 1903, even though lines like: "While she played, the sweet singer finger-ing the lute-strings, showing her skill to me/Ere the cock had crowed once, a first cup was quaffed by me" (29), sound extremely innocuous to the contemporary ear.

Jones, who translated these lines twice, obviously wavers between "moral blem-ishes." In prose he sides with Polk, and opts for a "blemish" of a sexual nature: "How often do I quaff pure wine in the morning, and draw towards me the fair lutani, whose delicate fingers skilfully touch the strings!" (10: 67–8). In verse, on the other hand, he sides with Johnson and prefers a "blemish" connected with drinking: "Sweet was the draught and sweet the blooming maid/Who touch'd her lyre beneath the fragrant shade;/We sip'd till morning purpled ev'ry plain;/The damsels slumber'd, but we sip'd again" (10: 343).

The same two polar attitudes can be observed in Western discourses on Islamic poetics. The *qasidahs* are dismissed by Wilson, who points out that "the essential qualities of Arabian poetry appear in the "Romance of Antar" and the tales of the "Thousand and One Nights" (49). Accordingly, he prints Labid's *qasidah* in Car-lyle's translation, which is not a translation of the whole *qasidah,* but merely of the *nasib,* or amatory prelude, calls the *qasidah* an "elegy" and supplies the reader with a summary of Labid's life in a footnote. A similar effect would be obtained if an editor of an anthology of English poetry were to dismiss the elegy as unimport-ant, print only the first thirty-two lines of Gray's *Elegy,* and give a potted version of Gray's life in a footnote.

Charles Tuetey, the most recent translator of Labid's *qasidah,* opts for basically the same strategy about eighty-five years later, with the not unimportant difference that he actually informs the reader of what he is doing: "Poem 18 by Labid is the ingress to his *Mu allaka.* It is the poet returning after years to the same spot, and remembering. A fine piece of nostalgic description, it lacks the dramatic concen-tration we find in Imrulkais, for instance" (18). Tuetey uses the term *mu allaka* to refer to the *qasidah.* In doing so he alludes to the (apocryphal) story that held that not just Labid's *qasidah* but the six other great *qasidahs,* or *mu allakat,* the plural, were cast in gold and suspended from the *kaabah* in Mecca – probably the most visually arresting example of canonization. Not only do Western readers who rely on Tuetey's anthology not get the whole *qasidah*; they are also invited to make a comparison between an author they have just been introduced to and another author they may never have heard of before and who is introduced to them in an equally fragmentary fashion.

Yet others rise to the defense of Islamic poetics, once they have acknowledged the possibility of its being different from Western poetics. The relativistic approach to poetics, which alone can lead to productive rewriting, is explicitly stated by Ilse Lichtenstadter: "However, our Western standards of what makes 'good' poetry do not suffice to appreciate the artistry [of Islamic poetry]. The native judgments of the respective merits use criteria that differ widely from ours" (26). But the relativistic approach has been implicit in many statements made by the more "progressive" rewriters of Islamic literature in the past. It is significant to observe that the statement just quoted was published in 1974. Lichtenstadter's book was published in paperback in 1975. By the same token, however, Wilson's anthology dismissing the *qasidahs* was republished unchanged in 1971.

Most defenses of Islamic poetics make use of the strategy of analogy mentioned above. To "justify" the fact that Islamic "epics" are written in a mixture of verse and prose, Carlyle enlists the help of the sacred book of his own culture by stressing that "from various parts of the Old Testament we may perceive that this mode of writing was practised among the Hebrews" (xii). This statement not only strongly suggests that what was good for the one must also be good for the other, but goes on to place the Semitic people which became fundamental to the development of "the West," not least through an immense operation of rewriting, on the same footing as the Semitic peoples which have, from 700 of the Common Era onwards, been seen as a threat to the same "West."

Carlyle goes even further and argues the superiority of the Arabic type of epic, in words anticipating Poe's attacks on the traditional Western epic:

> as in every poem of considerable length there must be trifling circumstances to relate, they were by this contrivance less liable to incur the ridicule which would arise from any incongruity betwixt a mean subject and a splendid diction, a ridicule from which neither the sublimity of the works of Homer nor the elegance of the Aeneid could entirely exempt their respective authors.
>
> (xiii)

In other words, the writers of the foundation epics of Western literature might have been grateful for the opportunity to use a mixed form used by Islamic poets as a matter of course.

One hundred and seventy-five years after Carlyle, Tuetey also makes use of the Homeric analogy, and also to justify the use of a certain diction. He writes that the "Arabian poets of the sixth century lived in the heroic age . . . comparable to that portrayed in Homer. This means directness, realism, striking detail, poetry that is as large as life" (9) even, presumably, when it deals with "mean subjects," since in the years which have elapsed between the publication of Carlyle's book and that of Tuetey's, Western thinking about the epic has changed again, not least because the successful rewriting of the epic by Pound and Williams, resulting in a type of epic that can be made productive again in contemporary literature, has firmly put the "traditional" epic inside the boundaries of history, there to be studied but no longer emulated.

About a hundred years after the publication of Carlyle's book, Blunt echoes his defense of Islamic poetics by stating that early poetry produced in the Islamic system can only be compared to "the lyrical portion of the older Hebrew scriptures" (ix). Like other rewriters, though, Blunt also finds it difficult to rewrite the *qasidah* convincingly in terms of the genres offered by Western poetics. Lyall puts the matter succinctly as follows: "the form and spirit of ancient Arabian poetry are very distinct, though it is not easy to bring it within the classes known to European criticism. It is not epic, nor even narrative . . . still less is it dramatic . . . the Greek idyll is perhaps the type which comes closest to it in Classical poetry" (xviii). Nicholson calls the *qasidah* an "ode" (76) in his *History,* and Jones writes about "casseida's or eclogues" (10: 341). The same Nicholson tries to sidestep the issue in his book of translations by declaring: "I disagree with the opinion that success may turn on the existence in the translator's language of a native form and manner corresponding" (viii), but adds rather lamely in the same breath: "but undoubtedly advantage should be taken of such models when possible" (viii). His analogy for the *qasidah* is the English verse narrative as pioneered by Scott and made popular by Byron.

To bring home to the reader in a most forceful manner the generic difference between the *qasidah* and anything extant in any Western literature, Arberry quotes at length from Ibn Qutaiba's *Poetry and Poets* in Nicholson's translation:

> I have heard from a man of learning that the composer of Odes began by mentioning the deserted dwelling places and the relics and traces of habitation. Then he wept and complained and addressed the desolate encampment, and begged his companions to make a halt, in order that he might have occasion to speak of those who had once lived there and afterwards departed; for the dwellers in tents were different from townsmen and villagers in coming and going, because they moved from one water-spring to another, seeking pasture and searching out the places where rain had fallen. Then to this he linked the erotic prelude, and bewailed the violence of his love and the anguish of separation from his mistress and the extremity of his passion and desire, so as to win the hearts of his hearers and divert their eyes towards him and invite their hearts to listen to him, since the song of love touches men's souls and takes hold of their hearts. . . . Now, when the poet had assured himself an attentive hearing, he followed up his advantage and set forth his claim: thus he went on to complain of fatigue and want of sleep and travelling by night and of the noonday heat, and how his camel had been reduced to leanness. And when, after representing all the discomfort and danger of his journey, he knew that he had his due meed from the person to whom the poem was addressed, he

entered upon the panegyric, and incited him to reward, and kindled his gen-
erosity by exalting him above his peers and pronouncing the greatest dignity,
in comparison with his, to be little.

(15–16)

Tuetey, on the other hand, is tempted to give up. He states in his introduction that
"it must be said that for an introduction to Arabic poetry the *Mu allakat* in their
present form are an unfortunate choice, the more so as they have diverted attention from much in pre-Islamic poetry that is both better preserved and superior"
(13) – at least from the contemporary Western point of view. Obviously very
aware of the challenge he has just issued to a long tradition of Islamic criticism
and scholarship, Tuetey looks for support to a relatively shorter-lived counter-
tradition, which declared the *mu allakat* to be spurious, as a whole or in part. He
does not go that far, but uses philological arguments to discredit and undermine
the place the *mu allakat* have occupied in the tradition of Islamic literature,
suggesting that since their authenticity is in doubt, their central position should
be as well, and forgetting, of course, that the reception of a work of literature
has nothing whatsoever to do with its "authenticity." As is well known, Goethe
enthused over *Ossian* and even translated parts of it. The fact that that text was a
total forgery did nothing at all to alter its – triumphant – reception in the Europe
of its time, nor does that fact change the historical importance of that text and
its reception in any way.

Tuetey tries to reinforce his point by reminding the reader that "successive
editors sought to bring them [*mu allakat*] up to 'standard length' by adding and
interpolating what other fragments in the same metre and rhyme they found in the
authors' works" (13). In other words, since the *mu allakat* are not authentic anyway, and since we know for a fact that "Hammad (of Kufa)," who was apparently
also responsible for the selection of the *mu allakat,* playing a part not unanalogous
to that played in Greek literature by the librarians of Alexandria, "was caught out
adding lines of his own to a poem by Zuhair" (13), why bother translating these
"fakes" at all? The real point, of course, is not whether the *qasidahs* in question
are authentic or not, but that they were perceived by a whole culture as close to the
pinnacle of canonization, and that it is strange, therefore, that they should remain
relatively unknown in other cultures.

Recent rewriters, who do not have recourse to the twin strategies of apology or
analogy, have succeeded in shedding light on the – to the Western reader – "peculiar" structure of the *qasidah.* They link that structure to the genesis of the genre
itself and the social conditions obtaining at that time, adding another obstacle in
the path of any attempt to transfer the *qasidah* from its native culture to another.
In ancient times, Ilse Lichtenstadter points out, "Near Eastern poetry was not
the expression of personal, individual, but of communal, religious emotions; it
performed a function within ancient society and its religious rites" (21). Andreas
Hamori seeks "other reasons" than those normally adduced for the "repetitive
tendency of the *qasida* and ritual is the one word that properly sums them up"

(21). W. R. Polk reminds the Western reader of the fact that the "audience was expected to break in at the end of each verse, to comment, to recite comparable verses, and to savor the artistry of the poet" (xxi), explaining both the – to the Western mind – "chaotic" structure of the *qasidah* and its lack of sequential narrative as defined in logical terms.

The Universe of Discourse familiar to the old Islamic poets, which is by no means familiar to the Western reader, presents another formidable obstacle to the reception of the *qasidah* in the West. Many elements belonging to that Universe of Discourse will fail to strike the Western reader as "fit to be mentioned in poetry." Carlyle translates the first *bayt* (a "verse" consisting of two – often longish – half-lines) as follows: "Those dear abodes which once contain'd the fair/Amidst Mitata's wilds I seek in vain/Nor towers, nor tents, nor cottages are there/But scatter'd ruins and a silent plain" (4). He goes on to translate the beginning of the second *bayt* as: "The proud canals that once Rayana grac'd" (4). Polk's comments on the translation of these *bayts* will serve admirably to illustrate the Universe of Discourse problems confronting prospective translators of the *mu allakat* and other *qasidahs*. "Carlyle," writes Polk, "who was familiar only with settled Arabs, thought Labid was referring to houses, and so he described the opening scene as a deserted Arabian village" (xvii). The original refers to an abandoned camp site in the desert, where "towers" and "cottages" would be hard to find, let alone decay to "scatter'd ruins." By the same token, what Carlyle takes to be "real" canals, conjuring up an image of Venice or Amsterdam, really refer to "flood channels, meaning the eroded gulleys that carry off the occasional rains" (Polk xxviii) – channels dug around the tents, in fact.

Significantly, later translators retain the "abodes" (Arberry 142) or change them into a "court" (Tuetey 117). Arberry specifies that the abodes are basically a "halting-place and encampment" (142), but Tuetey adds "dwellings" and even a "hearth" to his "court" (117). One reason for this may be that most recent translators of the *mu allakat* into English have indeed chosen to "adopt the romantic-exotic idiom established in the Victorian age" (Tuetey 8), referred to above. The alternative, according to Tuetey, would be to "fly off on a tangent, so to speak, and try to be avant-garde at all cost" (8).

Jones translates part of Labid's description of sunrise in the desert as: "the waking birds, that sung on ev'ry tree/Their early notes, were not so blithe as we" (343), totally overlooking the fact that the presence of birds, let alone trees, in the desert is rather unlikely, even though they are a staple of the "eclogues" he wanted to turn the *qasidahs* into. Nicholson drastically shortens the description of the camel in his translation of Labid, but without telling the reader so. Traditionally, the poets who produced early poetry in the Islamic system went to great lengths describing their camels, while proportionately devoting far fewer lines to the description of the women they loved. Western poetics has always tended to take a rather different view of proportions in this matter.

The last, but not least obstacle to the reception of the *qasidah* in the West is the very language it is written in, or rather, a combination of the properties of that language and the requirements of Islamic poetics. Gibb sums up the problem as follows:

> where the poet is held almost wholly to specific themes, and his aim is to embellish those themes with all the art at his command, to surpass his predecessors and rivals in beauty, expressiveness, terseness of phrase, in fidelity of description and grasp of reality, then such poetry can never be satisfactorily translated into any other language, just because the thing said varies so little and the whole art lies in the untranslatable manner of saying it.
>
> (22)

The main problem is that of the single end rhyme. Every *bayt* in the *qasidah* ends in the same sound. No translator into English has ever tried to keep it. Blunt writes: "it has therefore been decided to attempt neither the rhyme nor the terminal syllable, though advantage has been taken of all convenient occasions of conforming to the latter" (xxi). Nicholson made the same decision, though with fewer regrets: "Now and then I have copied the monorhyme of Oriental odes, but it is not easy to do so in poems of any length, nor is it worth the trouble" (1922: vii).

Both Nicholson and Blunt agree that "far more depends on the choice of a metre consorting with the tone, spirit, and movement of the original" (Nicholson 1922: viii). Unfortunately, this meter is, at least in Nicholson's case, often achieved only at the price of near or complete lack of intelligibility. It is hard to detect behind Nicholson's "Or as traceries on a woman's wrist, a tattoo of rings:/Pricked in with powdery soot the pattern sticks off distinct" (1922: 11) what Polk renders in honest prose as: "the renewing of a tattoo by the sprinkling and rubbing of soot in circles above which the tattoo appears" (19). Nicholson pays a high price for his "Arabic sprung rhythm," as does Blunt, who translates the same *bayt* as: "Scored with lines and circles, limned with rings and blazonings/as one paints a maid's cheek point-lined in indigo" (26). Arberry's translation of the same passage again reveals the extent of his dependence on the diction of his predecessors: "or the back and forth of a woman tattooing, her indigo/in rings scattered, the tattooing newly revealed above them" (142). Carlyle, obedient to the poetological constraints of his time, translates: "As the dust sprinkled on a punctur'd hand/Bids the faint tints resume their azure hue" (6), and has to make the sense clear in a footnote: "It is a custom with Arabian women, in order to give the veins of their hands and arms a more brilliant appearance, to make slight punctures along them, and to rub into the incisions a blue powder, which they renew occasionally as it happens to wear out" (6). The poetics of another time allow Tuetey to say much the same thing inside his translation of the actual poem: "as with indigo-blue the girl redraws/the faded patterns marking her palm" (117).

Both metrical padding and highly explanatory prose tend to dilute the power of the primordial feature of the early *qasidahs*: the image. No translator seems to have succeeded in solving the crucial problem that faces those who try to acculturate the *qasidah* in the West, namely: "to render this poetry in a form that is reasonably self-explanatory to the English reader while retaining the economy and compactness typical of pre-Islamic poetry" (Tuetey 8). Filshtinsky may point to one of the reasons why this should be so: "the poets discarded all that their hearers could supplement with the aid of their own imagination. This endowed their world with a concise, dynamic quality, and enabled the listener to perceive the image quickly and easily" (19).

The fault lies not only with the translator, but also with the wide divergence in Universes of Discourse: through no fault of their own, Western readers can supplement very little with the aid of their own imagination. The translator has to do it for them, traditionally by smuggling wordy explanations into the text, or by relying on footnotes. The translator can also try to recreate the image in another way, as W. R. Polk has done, by offering the reader a scholarly introduction, a literal translation, notes, and "finally, photographs" that "attempt to capture the mood presented in each verse" (viii): an abdication of the power of language, as the *Cambridge History of Arabic Literature* reminds us, to "translate from Arabic classics in a way attractive to a reader unacquainted with the original tongue and civilization associated with it" (x).

7 Translation: Universe of Discourse

"Holy Garbage, tho by Homer cook't"

The subtitle of this chapter is the phrase the Earl of Roscommon (d. 1685) uses in his *Essay on Translated Verse* to refer to the reluctance translators of his time displayed toward translating certain aspects of the Homeric Universe of Discourse: certain objects, customs, and beliefs thought unacceptable in their own culture. Based on a comparison of translations of the funeral of Patroclus (Iliad xxiii) and the martial exploits of Idomeneus (Iliad xiii), this chapter will explore translators' attitudes toward the Universe of Discourse expressed in the original text in relation to the Universe of Discourse of their own society.

This attitude is heavily influenced by the status of the original, the self-image of the culture that text is translated into, the types of texts deemed acceptable in that culture, the levels of diction deemed acceptable in it, the intended audience, and the "cultural scripts" that audience is used to or willing to accept.

The status of the source text can run the whole gamut from central to peripheral in either the source or the target culture. A text that is central in its own culture may never occupy the same position in another culture, as I have shown in the previous chapter by my analysis of attempts to acculturate the *qasidah*. In Homer's case it is safe to say that the Iliad was a central text in its own culture and became one of the central texts of West European culture (no matter what languages that culture made use of) until about Roscommon's time. In Macpherson's words: "The least impartial nations have contented themselves with giving the second place to the most favoured of their native poets. And to allow the first seat to Homer" (1: i).

The self-image of the target culture is by no means constant and unchangeable. A case may be made for the statement that a culture with a low self-image will welcome translation (and other forms of rewriting) from a culture or cultures it considers superior to itself. The culture of the French Renaissance, for instance, looks up to Homer without reserve. Its attitude persists in the rewritings of Homer – in the guise of both criticism and translation – authored by Madame Dacier.

The culture of the French eighteenth century, on the other hand, which thought of itself as having "come of age," no longer had the same unstinting admiration for the Iliad. Renaissance translators would translate Homer among other things also to interiorize the "rules," that is, the poetics of the epic, and to propagate them. They thought of classical Greek culture as the repository of those rules. By the eighteenth century, though, French culture considered itself superior to classical

Greek culture and thought of itself as the true guardian of the poetics of the West. Accordingly, De la Motte suggests that Homer should be judged by contemporary standards: "Quinault is openly condemned because he belongs to our century, and the favorable prejudice we have towards antiquity results in our not daring to feel Homer's faults" (197a).

By the eighteenth century the English also no longer considered Homer the supreme law-giver for all epic writing, nor did they continue to regard his epics as the touchstone against which all future epics should be tested. Rather, his stature is felt to exert a stifling influence on attempts to write those future epics: "The fetters, which the prevailing taste of modern Europe [shaped by those who unreservedly admire Homer] has imposed on poetry, may well be admitted as an excuse for a man of the best genius for not succeeding in the characteristic simplicity of Homer" (Macpherson xii).

In the French target culture of the seventeenth and eighteenth centuries, the epic as a genre, or type of literary text, no longer occupies the dominant position it did occupy during the Renaissance when Ronsard, for instance, painstakingly composed *La Franciade,* which remained and remains largely unread, simply because to be truly rated "great," a poet *had* to compose an epic. In the seventeenth and eighteenth centuries the epic lost its predominant position to the *tragédie,* and it is quite clear that De la Motte judges the epic by the standards of that *tragédie.* He makes this quite explicit in the introduction to his translation of the Iliad, which contains something like a "brief summary" of all that is needed in the *tragédie* and lacking in Homer:

> I have tried to make the narrative faster than it is in Homer, the descriptions larger and less burdened by details, the comparisons more exact and less frequent. I have freed the speeches from all I deemed contrary to the passion they express, and I have tried to introduce into them that gradual build-up of power and sense on which they depend for their greatest effect. Finally, I have seen to it that the characters are consistent, since the reader is likely to be most sensitive to that rule now so well known, and to judge most severely accordingly.
>
> (214b)

In England the situation is less clear-cut, owing to the stature of Milton's *Paradise Lost* as a national epic poem that is actually read, but the epic can be seen to begin to lose its dominant position there as well.

Diction suited to the composition of works of literature was very narrowly defined by the Académie in the French target culture of the seventeenth and eighteenth centuries. This extremely restricted diction made it very difficult for translators to include certain elements of the Homeric Universe of Discourse even if they wanted to go beyond the boundaries of the *agréable.* The words were simply not there. Or rather, the words were there, but the use of those words in a work of literature was not deemed acceptable. The mere use of this type of word would automatically condemn a translation to a subliterary existence, causing it to be rejected as "vulgar," no matter what its other virtues might be. Once more the situation is somewhat different in England, but middle- and late-Augustan poetic diction afford a definite analogy.

A "cultural script" could be defined as the accepted pattern of behavior expected of people who fill certain roles in a certain culture. The French people of the seventeenth century had a very definite cultural script for the role of "king." That script had been greatly elaborated on by Louis XIV. In no way could it be made to fit Homeric kings, most of whom would be seen by French people of *goût* to be living the lives of impoverished noblemen in their own day and age. In De la Motte's words:

> One does not see a multitude of officers or guards around the kings; the children of the sovereigns work in the gardens and guard the herds of their fathers; the palaces are definitely not superb, nor the tables sumptuous. Agamemnon dresses himself and Achilles prepares with his own hands the meal he gives to Agamemnon's ambassadors.
>
> (192b)

Similarly, where Homer's soldiers just sit about after they have put down the wood that will be used for Patroclus' funeral pyre, Madame Dacier explicitly makes them wait for orders, as a good soldier was supposed to do in the cultural script setting forth what good soldiers were to do in her time. In Macpherson's translation, Achilles does not just put the locks he has cut from his hair into the hands of the dead Patroclus: he does so neatly, as any good Scotsman would.

Since most seventeenth- and eighteenth-century translations of the Greek and Latin classics were made for people who knew Greek and Latin to some or even a considerable extent, the information value of the translation was rather low. In fact, a case could be made for not translating or "embellishing" certain aspects of the Homeric Universe of Discourse simply because most readers would be able to check what was left out or embellished in the original. Yet translations of the classics did have information value in one instance: if and when they were made for use in the classroom or to be read by young readers. In these cases, the translation would strictly be *ad usum Delphini.*

The translations of Homer written in France and England in and somewhat before Roscommon's time are still prephilological and relatively ahistorical in nature. They therefore illustrate both the problem of translating a Universe of Discourse and the strategies for solving that problem with a clarity ultimately rooted in the cultural naiveté that preceded cultural relativism in the West. During the period under consideration the image and prestige of the original, the Iliad, began to be questioned somewhat. Madame Dacier considers her translation a tribute to the genius of Homer; Houdar De la Motte considered his translation an attempt to make Homer palatable to the French readership of his time.

William Cowper writes in his introduction to his translation of the Iliad: "It is difficult to kill a sheep with dignity in a modern language" (xix). My contention is that language has absolutely nothing to do with it. If the original enjoys a highly positive reputation in the target culture, the translation is likely to be as literal as possible, which means that sheep will, indeed, be killed, whether with dignity or not. Or, in the words of Madame Dacier: "all that pertains to the customs must be kept" (1714: 359). When the image of the original is no longer uniformly positive in the target culture, more liberties are likely to be taken in translation, precisely because the original is no longer considered a "quasi-sacred" text: "As soon as morals became enlightened, as soon as philosophers appeared on the scene, we began to see criticism of Homer" (De la Motte 205b).

Once the original is no longer "taboo," the target culture begins to develop different attitudes toward it. The first of those attitudes consists of attempts to "justify" Homer. It is then said of the poet of the Iliad that: "He will appear to excel his own state of society, in point of decency and delicacy, as much as he has surpassed more polished ages in point of genius" (Wood 171). Even De la Motte is willing to admit that Homer is not responsible for the times he lived in: "In the dark times in which he lived he could not have had any healthy ideas of the Divinity, and whatever wit is imputed to him, he has not been able completely to avoid the contagion of the errors of Paganism and its absurdity" (189b). Fifty years later Bitaubé understands that there are readers who will reject Homer because "The more a nation is civilized, the more delicate its manners are, the more one is able to imagine that one might meet people in it who will have difficulty bowing to morals strongly opposed to those characteristics" (1: 29).

Another attitude is that of more or less complete acceptance of Homer on the basis of an awakening historicism. Madame Dacier writes: "I find the old times the more beautiful in that they resemble ours the less" (1713, 1: xxv). Yet she also tries to "justify" Homer against the taste of her own time by invoking the authority of the most central text of her culture that, paradoxically, turns out to be another translation: "He often speaks of cauldrons, of kettles, of blood, of fat, of intestines, etc. You see princes cut up the animals themselves and roasting them. People of the world find this shocking; but one must see that all of this totally conforms to what one sees in Holy Writ" (1: xxvi).

The different attitudes developed toward the original give rise to different translational strategies. Madame Dacier writes, quite predictably: "I confess that I have not tried to soften the power of his features to bring them closer to our century" (1713, 1: xxiii). On the other hand, Barbin, one of the early justifiers, states: "I have made use of general terms that are more congenial to our language than all those details, particularly with regard to certain things that seem too low to us today" (11). Finally, De la Motte puts the argument in favor of the neoclassical rules he had so perfectly interiorized: "I wanted my translation to be pleasing; I have therefore had to substitute ideas that are pleasing today for other ideas that were pleasing in Homer's time" (212b).

The genre that is dominant in the target culture defines to a great extent the readers' horizon of expectation with regard to the translated work that tries to take its place in that target culture. If it does not conform to the demands of the genre that dominates the target culture its reception is likely to be rendered more difficult, hence Madame Dacier's lament: "Most people now are spoilt by the reading of vast quantities of vain and frivolous books and they find themselves unable to bear with what is not written in the same taste" (1713, 1: v). Accordingly, these people tend to expect "heroes belonging to the bourgeoisie, always so polished, sweet and correct" (1: vi). Needless to say this type of hero is not likely to be found in the Iliad.

Hobbes remarks that: "the names of instruments and tools of artificers, and words of art, though of use in the Schools, are far from being fit to be spoken by a hero" (iv). More than a hundred years later Bitaubé echoes Madame Dacier. Readers' expectations have changed, and the new expectations determine the attitude with which they will be reading the translation of the Iliad: "The novels have, in part, accustomed us to wanting everything in a hero to be heroic" (1: 23). Because Homer's heroes are so different, and Homeric customs so unpalatable to the audience of his own time, De la Motte quite logically states: "for these reasons have I reduced the twenty-four books of the Iliad to twelve, which are even much shorter than Homer's" (213a/b), even though he has done more than his best to make the heroes of the Iliad behave in the manner his audience wanted them to behave: "I have left the Gods their passions, but I have tried to invest them with dignity always. I have not stripped the heroes of that unjust pride in which we often find grandeur, but I have cut away from them the avarice and the greed that lowers them in our eyes" (214b).

Generic expectations nurtured by the dominant genre also affect the composition of the translation. For De la Motte the *tragédie* is the central genre of the poetics of his time and culture. He therefore quite logically proceeds to rethink and recast the Iliad in terms of that *tragédie,* and justifies his strategy by an explicit appeal to what his audience is likely to expect from a *tragédie.* "Would spectators in the theater submit to being told during the pauses in a *tragédie* all that is going to happen in the next act? Would they approve of the action of the principal characters being interrupted by the affairs of *confidants*? Certainly not" (214a).

Generic expectations are likely to be somewhat different in different cultures. The introduction to an English translation of the Iliad, almost contemporary with De la Motte's French translation, has this to say of the French alexandrine: "French versification, especially of the Heroic sort, is intolerably tedious" (Ozell 4). What is the epitome of style and elegance for De la Motte is nothing of the kind to his British contemporaries. On the contrary, they conclude that "the drone of a bagpipe affords every whit as much Harmony" (Ozell 6), which should not really come as a surprise from the pen of British scholars who pronounce the French language "certainly the unfittest for Heroic Subjects" (Ozell 4), thus effectively challenging the right of the French to translate Homer at all and advancing the British claim to be the true successor to the "glory that was Greece."

The intended audience also plays a part in determining strategies for the translation of Universe-of-Discourse features. If Homer is translated for the young, as he often was in those stages of cultures which relied mainly, if not exclusively, on the book to propagate cultural values, certain aspects of his Universe of Discourse are likely to be omitted. In Bitaubé's words: "I have not lost from sight the education of the young and of those who want to study Homer in the original. A faithful translation that is not barbaric may make this study much easier" (1: 47).

And so to the translations. The Greek noun *enorchēs* means "he-goat" and is obviously associated with the adjective *enorchos* defined by Lidell and Scott as: "with the testicles in, uncastrated." Goats do not enjoy the best of reputations in the cultural script of the target culture(s) of the seventeenth, eighteenth, and nineteenth centuries (even in the twentieth century the Loeb Classical Library translates *enorchēs* as: "rams, males without blemish"). Accordingly, Rochefort translates it as "taureaux" (bulls), not because he does not know Greek or did not bother to look up the word, but because his cultural script calls for the sacrifice of an animal considered more noble than a mere goat. Bitaubé turns the he-goats into "béliers" (rams), but does not specify any further, presumably because the Homeric details are not likely to edify the young overmuch. Barbin probably adheres most closely to the cultural script of his day – if not to the original he is translating – by rendering "enorchēs" as "agneaux" (lambs), thus effectively rendering the Greek custom less barbaric.

One Homeric cultural script De la Motte is definitely unable to accept is that of the fairly elaborate description of wounds executed with "an anatomical precision that chills the imagination" (195a) of anyone used to an eighteenth-century script that relies heavily on euphemisms to describe any parts of the body. Accordingly, De la Motte reduces the nearly two hundred lines in the thirteenth book of the Iliad in which Homer describes the exploits of Idomeneus, his allies, and his adversaries in graphic detail to no more than two lines in his translation: "Idoménée, Ajax, Ménélas, Mérionne/De meurtres et de sang assouvissent Bellone" [Idomeneus, Ajax, Menelaos, Merion/Satisfy Bellona with murders and with blood] (245a).

One description in the thirteenth book of the Iliad is likely to shock the seventeenth- and eighteenth-century reader in both France and England more than all others. Meriones, the Greek hero, pursues Adamas, who fights on the Trojan side, and wounds him with his spear "aidoioon te mesegu kai omphalou, entha malista/ gignet'Arès alegeinos oizuroisi brotoisin" (lines 568–9) (between the genitals and the navel where cruel Ares becomes worst to unhappy mortals). Only Hobbes and Cowper even try to translate the original in full. Cowper writes: "the shame between/And navel pierced him, where the stroke of Mars/Proves painful most to miserable man" (255), rendering the genitals by the more decorous "shame," but mentioning them at least, as does Hobbes by means of a similar circumlocution: "Meriones sent after him a spear,/Which ent'ring at his hinder parts, came out/ Beneath his navel, and above his gear/Where wounds most fatal are" (155). Yet the euphemism "gear," which also fits the rhyme, is offset by the addition of the graphic description of the path the spear pursues through the body of Adamas. Among French translators Rochefort resorts to zero translation, leaving out the offending lines altogether. The others use various circumlocutions.

Barbin simply writes: "Le fer estoit entré fort avant" [the iron had entered very far in the front] (296), probably with the intention of making the reader think of a nobler place, like the chest, in which the spear might have entered. Madame Dacier is more daring: she has the spear enter somewhat lower, "au milieu du corps" [in the middle of the body], and goes on to add: "justement dans l'endroit où les blessures sont les plus douloureuses et les plus mortelles" [precisely at the spot where wounds are the most painful and the most lethal] (1713, 2: 289). The studied vagueness of the wording makes it possible for the reader to think of the stomach as well as of the genitals, and bend the passage to fit his or her cultural script with minimal revulsion. Bitaubé has the spear enter "sous le nombril, où les atteintes de Mars sont fatales aux malheureux mortels" [under the navel, where the blows of Mars are fatal to unfortunate mortals] (2: 21), localizing the wound fairly accurately without stooping to further details. The other English translators referred to here, Ozell and Macpherson, have each adopted a similar strategy, albeit one hundred, and fifty years apart. Ozell has: "Below his Navel plung'd his fatal Spear, Where the least Wound inflicts a certain Death" (145–6). Macpherson translates: "Below the navel he struck him with force: Where death enters, with fatal ease" (2: 33).

Actual descriptions of a kind not deemed admissible in a cultural script confront translators with a definite challenge when they try to translate Universe-of-Discourse elements. Yet the problems are by no means limited to descriptions of "real" things: they also surface in the case of "literary" devices such as the simile. The Trojan hero Harpalion, pierced by the same Greek hero Meriones, but this time with an arrow, dies in the arms of his comrades and "hoos te skoolēks epi gaiē/keito tatheis" [like a worm on the earth he lay stretched out] (lines 654–5). Rochefort objects to the vulgar image of the worm and resorts, once again, to zero translation: "Frappé par Mérion d'un coup inattendu,/Il tombe et se débat, dans la poudre étendu" [Hit by Merion with an unexpected blow/He falls and writhes, stretched out in the powder] (255). "Se débat," though somewhat graphic, may still be said to fall within the bounds of acceptable diction, and "la poudre" (powder) takes the place of the less decorous "poussière" (dust).

Madame Dacier translates "la poussière," but omits the worm in the text of her translation, only to mention it in a footnote. Her translation reads: "Il estoit estendu sur la poussière" [he was stretched out on the dust] (1713, 2: 294). The footnote apologizes: "Le Grec dit, *il estoit estendu comme un ver sur la poussière* [the Greek says: he was stretched like a worm on the dust], and goes on to dismiss the simile as a "comparaison basse" [simile of a low kind], that "ne réussirait pas en nostre langue" [would not be successful in our language] (2: 567). The simile's success or lack thereof has nothing to do with the language as such but with the cultural script to which the users of that language subscribe. It is remarkable that Madame Dacier, who makes a point of translating Homer as literally as possible, parts company with him here. She does not seem to have realized that the analogy with Holy Writ, which she herself mentioned in her critical text on Homer, might have worked in this passage too. After all, Christ is likened to a worm in a passage designed to foreground the utter wretchedness of the human condition. Barbin, who may have realized the potential of the analogy, translates: "et il demeura étendu, comme un ver de terre que l'on a écrasé" [and he stayed stretched out, like an earthworm that people have crushed] (299), even heightening the impact of the simile as he does so.

The fact that Barbin and Madame Dacier seem to have switched roles here is further proof of the importance of the "human factor" in translation and other kinds of rewriting. Like great Homer, the translator also nods, overlooks, makes mistakes. But there is a fundamental difference between this type of mistake and the mistakes triumphantly held up to ridicule in certain normative writings on translation. This kind of writing would summarily dismiss De la Motte's translation of the Iliad as "not a translation at all" and, in doing so, rid itself of fascinating material for the analysis of the evolution and development of literatures, simply because De la Motte's text does not conform to a time-bound concept of translation fixated exclusively on the original. An approach to translation which rests content with decreeing which translations ought to exist and which ought not is very limited indeed. Rather, it should analyze texts which refer to themselves as translations and other rewritings and try to ascertain the part they play in a culture. The sheer number of rewritings should alert writers on translation of this ilk to the fact that they may not be dealing adequately with the matter at hand, just as the repeated and regular incidence of what they refer to as "mistakes" ought to alert them to the fact that an isolated mistake is, probably, just that, whereas a recurrent series of "mistakes" most likely points to a pattern that is the expression of a strategy.

Unlike Madame Dacier, Bitaubé mentions the worm but elevates it to a higher rank within the animal kingdom: his Harpalion "s'étend à terre comme un reptile" [stretches himself on the ground like a reptile] (2: 24). Among the English translators Ozell resorts to zero translation, whereas Macpherson translates literally: "Stretcht on earth, like a worm, he lay" (2: 35). Cowper also translates literally: "And like a worm lay on the ground" (258), whereas Hobbes has to "benumb" the worm in his translation in order not to fall short of the requirements of the meter he has imposed on it. He translates: "And lay like to a worm benumbed that/Upon the ground itself at length extends" (157).

A final, obvious example of the influence of cultural script on the translation of Universe-of-Discourse elements is to be found in the twenty-third book of the Iliad. After he has lit the funeral pyre of his friend Patroclus, Achilles sacrifices "doodeka de Trooon megathumoon ueias esthlous/chalkooi dēioon; kaka de phresi mēdeto erga" [twelve noble sons of the great-hearted Trojans/with bronze cutting down; bad the work he intended in his heart] (lines 175–6). Rochefort turns the two lines into four and writes: "Il accomplit enfin son projet détestable/Il s'élance, et, d'un glaive armant son bras coupable/Dans le sang malheureux de douze Phrygiens/Il trempe, sans pitié, ses homicides mains" [He accomplishes at last his detestable project/He throws himself forward and, arming his guilty arm with a sword/In the unhappy blood of twelve Phrygians/He dips, without pity, his homicidal hands] (262–3). Not surprisingly, the passage has the diction of the *tragédie*. The bronze becomes "un glaive" and Achilles actually dips his hands in the blood of the victims – an action that may have seemed barbaric to the Homeric Greeks themselves, but was obviously acceptable to Rochefort's audience that had read Plutarch on the assassination of Julius Caesar. In fact, Rochefort's audience may well have projected the last years of Republican Rome back on the Greeks of Homer's time, replacing one cultural script by another.

In Bitaubé the bronze becomes "fer" (iron) and the evil in Achilles' heart becomes the much more standardized "couroux, que rien ne pouvait arrêter" [wrath that nothing could stop] (2: 382). Barbin remains vague: Achilles simply selects twelve Trojans and "leur fit perdre la vie" [made them lose their lives] (521), without any gory details. Going against her stated principles once again, Madame Dacier tries to weaken the violence of the original, probably also in an attempt to make Achilles a more "positive" hero, by supplying the reader with the rules of the cultural script in which that violence takes place. She translates: "Enfin, pour achever d'apaiser l'ombre de son ami, il immole douze jeunes Troyens des plus vaillants et des meilleures familes, car l'excès de sa douleur et un désir de vengeance ne lui permettait pas de garder aucune modération" [Finally, to appease the shade of his friend, he immolates twelve young Trojans of the most valiant and of the best families, for the excess of his pain and a desire for vengeance did not allow him to keep any moderation] (1713, 3: 297).

8 Translation: language

Catullus' many sparrows

Texts, both original and translated, achieve, or at least intend to achieve, their effect on their readers in a number of ways. The final effect is usually achieved through a combination of "illocutionary strategies" or ways to make use of linguistic devices. Readers of translated texts not infrequently expect the combination of illocutionary strategies to be less effective in the translation than in the original. They will, if not actively expect, at least resign themselves to the fact that "something gets lost" in the translation.

What gets lost, not infrequently to the same extent in both original texts and translations, is the "ideal combination" of illocutionary strategies, the – admittedly rather shadowy, but nonetheless effective – concept that "the text could have been better" – written or rewritten. Readers who are able to compare the original and a number of translations, as the present reader is about to do in this chapter, are often also able to point out why the "ideal combination" of illocutionary strategies has not been achieved in the translation. The reason is often to be found in the simple fact that one strategy is privileged above others in the translation, and that this is felt to result in what is often described as "awkwardness, woodenness, lack of style," not for reasons grounded in the text of the original as such, but for reasons extrinsic to the text. One reason is the difference between the languages in which the original and the translation have been expressed; the other reason is the dominant "poetics" of translation at the time a particular translation is made. Many nineteenth-century translations of Catullus' second poem, for instance, which will be briefly discussed here, rhyme, even though the original does not.

The need to rhyme, therefore, by no means comes out of the "structure" of the original; quite the contrary. It is imposed on translators by the "translation poetics" of their day, which in the nineteenth century held that acceptable poetry translations should make use of the illocutionary strategies of meter and rhyme. Translation poetics, like all poetics, tend to change over the years. Languages also change, but most often not in any way that reduces their differences: the difference between Latin and nineteenth-century English has not become appreciably less than that between Latin and twentieth-century English. Whereas translators, then, do have some recourse against the constraints of the translation poetics of their time, they have absolutely no recourse against the difference between the language of the original and that of the translation.

Languages are different, and no amount of translator training is ever likely to reduce that difference. Translator training can, however, alert translators both to the relativity of translation poetics and to strategies that may be used not to "overcome" the differences between languages, which are an undeniable given, but to project "their" image of the original, which may be influenced by various considerations, not just of ideology and/or poetics, but also of the intended audience of the translation. These strategies are by no means limited to the realm of linguistics alone. Rather, they operate on the level of ideology, poetics, Universe of Discourse, *and* linguistics.

The translation poetics of a given period in a given culture often forces translators to privilege one or two illocutionary strategies at the expense of others. Rhyme and meter have already been mentioned above in the case of nineteenth-century translations. The other privileged illocutionary strategy is, of course, that of the word, the desire to enshrine lexical equivalence (the celebrated "word for word") as the kingpin of the whole translation process, the central element that would guarantee the much desired "fidelity."

Hence the quandaries expressed in most writing on the translation of literature. Hence also its repetitiveness and lack of productivity. Translators, we are likely to be told, will be able to render the sense of the original only at the expense of the sound, and often also of the morphosyntactic features organizing the original. If they want to render the sound, they will find it hard to salvage the sense, and their translation will often be dismissed as a mere exotic curiosum. If they try to impose the morphosyntactic surface structure of the source language on the target text, they will in all probability lose whatever elegance and balance the original may have possessed in that respect.

Most writing on translation has elevated what are, basically, simple and inescapable facts rooted in the very difference of languages and in the dictates of translation poetics to the loftier status of "problems," often said to defy any kind of solution, or to be capable of solution only after some – preferably "titanic" and protracted – "struggle against the limitations of language." The problem tends to disappear – or, even better, to allow of attempts at solution that may be said to be "productive" to the extent that they open a wider horizon not just for the study of translations as such, but for their insertion into a concept of literary theory closely connected with comparative literature – as soon as the only reason for the problem's existence that can disappear does so: as soon as the translation poetics is no longer normative but descriptive in nature – as soon as it no longer consists of a series of prescriptions, but of descriptions of possible strategies translators can make use of and have made use of.

There is one level on which translation remains a prescriptive operation: translators would be well advised to bow to the dictates of the dictionary, and not translate Catullus' "passer" (swallow) by "hippopotamus," for instance. The very nature of the example indicates that this level is trivial indeed in relation to the discussion we are engaged in here. Translators should know the grammars and the lexica – the "locutionary" aspects – of the languages they want to work with before they begin to translate. Translation training should not be designed to teach potential translators languages, but the illocutionary strategies inherent in those languages. Prospective translators should already possess the necessary locutionary skills.

In what follows, I propose to outline a short catalogue of illocutionary strategies used by translators over the past two centuries to project their image of Catullus' second poem for their culture, or at least for certain readerships in that culture. To show that these strategies are fairly constant through time and can be systematized with relative ease, I shall conduct the discussion of the translations not in chronological, but in alphabetical order. It should also be noted that many of the translations make use of the same two or three strategies. I have therefore limited myself to the most striking examples only.

But first, the text:

> Passer, deliciae meae puellae,   1
> quicum ludere, quem in sinu tenere,
> cui primum digitum dare appetenti
> et acres solet incitare morsus
> cum desiderio meo nitenti   5
> carum nescio quid lubet iocari,
> credo ut, cum gravis acquiescet ardor,
> sit soliaculum sui doloris,
> tecum ludere sicut ipsa possem
> et tristis animi levare curas!   10

A translation on the locutionary level might read:

> Sparrow, delight of my girl, with whom she is wont to play, whom she is wont to hold in her lap, to whom, who is trying to reach [her], she is wont to give the tip of her finger, whom she is wont to incite to sharp bites when it pleases my shining desire to play with something dear, I know not what, I believe in order for it to be a small solace for her grief when the heavy desire subsides. If I could only play with you as she does and lighten the sad cares of my soul!

Needless to say, this translation has ruthlessly privileged both the semantic (word for word) and the morphosyntactic components of the original.

It should be pointed out at the outset that the original could have been better written: the syntax of lines 6 and 7 is not clear. Syntax, the morphosyntactic difference between Latin and English, confronts translators with the main organizational problem of their text. Some, as we shall see later, project the morphosyntax of Latin on English; others opt for English syntax. The problem is represented in the translation given above by the repetition of "is wont to." Latin allows the verb "solet" (line 4) to control the verbs "ludere," "tenere" (both in line 2), and "incitare" (in line 4) in such a way that "solet" itself needs to be expressed only once. Furthermore, the inflected nature of Latin allows "Passer" (line 1) to be followed by four appositions, each in a different case: "deliciae," vocative, line 1, "quicum," instrumental, line 2, "quem," accusative, line 2, and "cui," dative, line

3. Latin also allows for an apposition to an apposition: "appetenti" is an apposition to "cui" in line 4. In English, the cases are normally rendered by prepositions, to the detriment of the urgency expressed in the Latin.

Translators are further confronted with the problem of connotation on the semantic level: "deliciae" in line 1 carried the connotation of "love making" in the "trendy" jargon of Catullus' time. "[S]oliaculum" in line 8 is a neologism, coined especially for this poem, not a word in current usage. "[I]psa" in line 9 carries overtones of "mistress." Kenneth Quinn, to whose commentary I am heavily indebted, points out that slaves used to refer to their masters as "ipse" [himself] (94). "[A]rdor" in line 7 means the "desire for the beloved" and is paired in line 8 with "dolor" (in the genitive, "doloris"), which suggests the "pining" for the absence of the beloved. "[C]arum" in line 6, "dear," also has overtones of "precious," and "appetenti" in line 3, here said of the sparrow, is normally reserved to describe the action of a man kissing a woman's hand.

None of the translators to be discussed here tried to render the connotations of "deliciae" and "appetenti." Similarly, no translators tried to move beyond the intra-textual to the textual and contextual level. Quinn points out that the original is a parody of a formal hymn to a god or goddess, which explains both the string of appositions (the epithets with which the god[dess] is usually addressed) and the concluding "prayer" of the last two lines. On the contextual level, Sappho represents Aphrodite as riding a chariot drawn by horses, which may explain why Catullus gives Lesbia a sparrow for a pet, otherwise an unlikely choice indeed, even in late Republican Rome.

In contrast, many translators attempt to carry over some of the phonological properties of the original: the repetition of sounds like "p," "k" (spelled both [q] and [c]), "d," "o," "ae" (pronounced [ai]), and "i" knits the lines of the poem together in such a way that enjambements appear smooth and natural, and an impression of speed and urgency is created, only to be dashed in the last two lines.

Just as the semantic component of the original is reduced to mere denotational word-for-word correspondence in many translations, so the generic component of the original is, in many cases, reduced to mere attempts to recreate or approximate its meter or to replace it with a formal meter considered equivalent to it in English versification. It is hard to find more eloquent proof not only of the existence, but also of the tremendous influence of translation poetics or what Gideon Toury has been untiringly calling "translational norms" over the past decade.

But now to the translations. Arthur Symons's translation reprinted by W. A. Aiken (57) helps us understand why many translations that profess to be "literal" differ among themselves nevertheless. The reason is not to be sought in the different dictionaries translators use, but in what they imagine. Not unlike Isidore of Seville they try to reconcile what they read in the text and the dictionary with what they see in their environment. Mia Vannerem and Mary Snell-Hornby introduce Charles Fillmore's "scenes-and-frames" concept into translation analysis. The "frame" is the linguistic form on the page, the "scene" the reader's (translator's) personal experience that allows him or her to relate to the frame. Vannerem and Snell-Hornby point out that the translator does possibly not activate the same *scenes* a native speaker of the language would activate, or the scenes the author intended, because the *scenes* activated by a *frame* are very closely linked to the socio-cultural background of the language user in question.

(190)

"[S]inu" in line 2 of the original, means little more than "a fold or curve in the body or in one's dress" (92). Symons translates it as "bosom" obviously activating a different "scene." He calls Lesbia "my bright/Shining lady of delight" in an attempt to use the strategy of compensation. He had translated "deliciae" in line 1 as the much more neutral "darling," and tries to "make amends" by slipping in the cognate later on in his translation. He also manages to keep one parallelism of the original, both on the semantic and the phonological level by rendering the opposition "ardor:dolor" as: "Love's full ardours being over/She may find some after-staying/Of the heart-ache."

Copley consciously uses another "scene" to recreate the – at least initially – playful mood of the original. He renders lines 3 and 4 as: "or sticks out a finger – oo, you little rascal/you peck, go on do it again, harder, oo" (2). He also uses the strategy of explicitation in his rendering of the last two lines, offering the reader both what is there in the original *and* his own interpretation of that original: "I'd like to play the way she does/and soothe within my heart the ache of love." It will have become obvious that he does not attempt a metrical translation in the traditional sense. Instead, his deliberate recasting of Catullus in terms of a more modernist poetics may well be seen as an attempt to approximate the function Catullus' own innovative poems had in the poetry of his day.

Lesbia has become a "nymph," rather than a girl in Elton's "scene" as printed in Kelly's collection (170). He goes a step beyond "scene" or, rather, uses a scene that has petrified into a cliché in the cultural script of his time when he translates "sinu" as "the soft orbings of her breast." He makes use of the same clichés on the level of diction in his translation of the last two lines: "I would that happy lady be,/And so in pastime sport with thee,/And lighten love's soft agony" – in which the first line has been dictated by the strategy of explicitation.

Goold tries to project the morphosyntactic structures of the original on the English language: "O sparrow that are my sweetheart's pet,/with whom she likes to play, whom to hold in her lap,/to whose pecking to offer her finger-tips/and provoke you to bite sharply" (33). He also makes use of the explicitation strategy, making Lesbia "bright-eyed with longing for me" – the last two words are not stated in the original.

Gregory slips a literary allusion to a well-known work in English literature into his translation of the last line of the original, either as a veiled attempt at explicitation, or possibly as an attempt to compensate for the loss of the literary allusion contained in the "sparrow" of the original. His last line reads: "This pastime/would raise my heart from darkness" (4).

William Hull tries to come up with an "equivalent" for Catullus' "soliaculum" and translates line 8 as: "she finds a pain in miniature/and defined a precise relief"

(4). The Latin diminutive is expressed in terms of a different grammatical category (a preposition followed by a noun), which is applied not to the relief but to the pain, and since the relief is probably commensurate to the pain it, too, is conceivably thought of by the reader as "in miniature." The strategy of switching grammatical categories is a relatively common one among translators. Often, as here, function morphemes (mostly affixes) are replaced by content morphemes such as nouns and adjectives. Hull obviously tries not to translate the last two lines by any of the clichés that have become the staple of Western love poetry between the time when Catullus wrote his original and 1968. Hull's last lines read: "could introduce precision of light/into my weight of night."

Kelly translates Catullus' second poem into prose, and finds in this fact an additional incentive to project the morphosyntactic features of Latin on English. The result is not unlike Goold's attempt in verse: "Sparrow, delight of my girl, which she plays with, which she keeps in her bosom, to whose eager beak she offers the tip of her finger" (9–10). Kelly also explicitates. Unlike many other translators he indicates that he does so by underlining the explicitation. "Dolor" becomes "the grief *of absence*" in his translation. The reason he underlines his explicitation and attempts what amounts to a morphosyntactic calque must most likely be sought in the audience to which the "Bohn Classical Library," in which his volume appeared, addressed itself: students and anyone wishing to study the classics in "literal" translations.

Lamb, whose translation is reprinted in Kelly (170), tries to combine a projection of Latin morphosyntactic structures on English with the maintenance of a fairly strict rhyme-scheme. The result reads as follows:

> Dear sparrow, long my fair's delight,
> > Which in her breast to lay,
> To give her finger to whose bite,
> Whose puny anger to excite
> > She oft is wont in play.

The "scene" the last two lines activate in Lamb is obviously somewhat different from the one imagined by Catullus. In the original it is nowhere stated that Lesbia is "away," but Lamb definitely opts for this interpretation: "Assuage my pangs when she's away,/And bring relief to me."

Jack Lindsay changes grammatical categories in his translation of Catullus' first line: "Sparrow, my girl delights in you" (no page) and makes use of the strategy of circumlocution to express his own "scene" of line 2: "and in her breast's deep nest of warmth/motherly set you."

Theodore Martin published two versions of Catullus' second poem in his collection of translations. In his first version he is forced to use padding in order to fulfill the demands of both meter and rhyme. Many of his fellow translators are forced to make use of the same strategy, but I have not quoted from them at any length here since Martin's translation itself is such an obvious example of the process. Martin's translation of Catullus' lines 1–3 reads: "Sparrow, that art my darling's pet –/My darling's, who'll frolic with thee and let/Thee nestle in her bosom, and when/Thou peck'st her forefinger will give it again" (4). The same demands also force him to oblige with verbosity in translating lines 5 and 6 as: "When that glorious creature who rules my heart/Enchants it all the more with her playful wiles." He also tries to compensate within the totality of Catullus' oeuvre. Instead of resorting to the usual clichés to render the last two lines, he writes: "And lighten the pangs that are rending me," an obvious allusion to the "excrucior" (I am torn apart) in what is perhaps Catullus' most famous poem: "Odi et amo."

In his second version, Martin imagines a "scene" in which Catullus is somewhat closer to the Victorian suitor watching the girl of his dreams play with the canary she has just taken from its cage. In this second version lines 5 and 6 of the original become: "When she is minded, that lady whom I dote on,/Pretty tricks to play, all maddeningly charming" (5). Martin's "lady whom I dote on" points out another strategy translators are often forced to fall back on by the demands of rhyme and meter: that of "flattening": the illocutionary power of the original is sacrificed in favor of mere locutionary communication.

James Michie makes use of protracted enjambement to recapture the speed and fluency of the original, as well as the lightness of its tone. Lines 2 to 4 read in his translation: "Her playmate whom she loves to let/Perch in her bosom and then tease/With tantalising fingertips/Provoking angry little nips" (19).

Raphael and McLeish change the syntactic pattern of the original in an attempt to convey its mood. The Latin address is turned into an English question. Lines 1 and 2 in Catullus, for instance, become: "Well, little sparrow, who's my darling's darling then?/Does she like to play with it and hold it in her lap?" (25). They also resort to morphemic repetition to capture the lighthearted diction of the first half of the original. Lines 3 and 4 read in their translation: "Does she get it to stretch its beak/To tip her fingertip – provoke the little pecker's peck?"

Carl Sesar renders the Latin address, which is expressed by means of the vocative case in the original, by means of the obvious English word: "Hello, sparrow" (no page). He pads his fifth line to bow to the demands of meter: "And glows, lovely, her eyes flashing," and he subjects his eighth line to the same treatment: "once the heavy burning need dies down."

C. H. Sisson resorts to etymology to render lines 7 and 8 of the original in a way that is intelligible to the English-speaking reader while remaining close to the Latin: "(I think, when her grave fire acquiesces/She finds it a solace for her pain)" (11).

R. A. Swanson imagines the following "scene" to render "sinu" in line 2: "permits to lie/within her lap" (3). J. F. Symons-Jeune again imagines a different scene for "sinu": "clasps thee to her neck" (5). She also conforms to the cultural script of both Antiquity and the 1920s by making Lesbia's fingertip "rosy," whereas the original leaves its color unspecified.

J. H. A. Tremenheere once again imagines a different scene: his sparrow is more violent in its behavior than Catullus'. His translation of line 4 reads: "To tempt thy sallies and excite/Many a cruel, cruel bite!" His "scene reading" of Lesbia, on the other hand, comes close to that provided by Martin: "Since petty follies such as these/My sweetheart exquisite can please" (39).

A. S. Way changes the Latin vocative into a full-fledged English sentence: "Sparrow, I cry you greeting" (1). His "scene" of Lesbia's playing with the bird is different once again: "And 'twixt her palms enfolds you" (2) is nowhere to be found in the Latin original. The same scene makes him also add two lines in which "she [Lesbia] scolds you [bird]/With laughing lip" (2).

Peter Whigham compensates in a way that is different from any we have discussed until now. By explicitly calling the sparrow: "Lesbia's sparrow," he historicizes the original, folding the many centuries of reception back into the poem itself. He also uses etymology to stay close to the Latin while rendering Catullus' neologism in an acceptable manner. His translation of line 8 reads: "a little solace for her satiety" (8).

F. A. Wright has perhaps the most daringly historicizing reading of the opening of the original. His first line squarely transplants Lesbia's bird to middle-class England. It reads: "My darling's canary, her plaything, her pet" (94). His Lesbia takes her place with Martin's and Tremenheere's in the ranks of ethereal young ladies playing absent-mindedly with their canaries: "She lets you for warmth in her soft bosom linger,/And smiles when you peck at the tip of her finger" (95). The "warmth," though compatible with the scene Wright contextualizes, may also have been rendered necessary by the demands of meter. In the original, Catullus' Lesbia certainly never smiles.

Though many translators try to approximate Catullus' phonological effects, Celia and Louis Zukofsky are the only ones who explicitly privilege the phonological level of the original in their attempts to translate it. Their unabashed attempt to render the sound, rather than the sense, flew in the face of the translation poetics of their time, and their translation has, accordingly, never achieved more than a certain notoriety as a curiosum doomed not to be taken seriously. Line 7 of the original becomes "I think, it is the crest of passion quieted," the second half of which actually mimics the sounds of the Latin with some degree of success, as do the final lines: "could I but lose myself with you as she does,/breathe with a light heart, be rid of these cares" (no page).

Summing up, an analysis of the tradition shows that the translators of Catullus 2 have provided the reader with sometimes widely diverging scenes activated by the same frame. They have made use of the following strategies that have remained remarkably constant: phonological approximation, compensation, explicitation, the use of cliché both on the level of diction and of cultural script, morphosyntactic projection of the original language on the language of the translation, morphosyntactic switching and switching of grammatical categories, rhyme and meter, the attempt to create neologisms, circumlocution, padding and verbosity, "flattening," that is, reduction of illocutionary effect, morphemic repetition, and the use of etymological cognates.

It is not my intention here to evaluate the different translations. Nor is it my task to do so: evaluation would simply reveal the hidden prescriptive assumptions with which I approach the translations. Since I have tried to describe, not prescribe, there is no reason why I should evaluate. That task is better left to the reader.

I merely hope to have shown in this chapter that a descriptive analysis of translations on the linguistic level can be productive in terms of translator training, and in the previous chapters that a descriptive analysis of translations on the mere linguistic level does not even begin to do justice to the complexity of the phenomenon.

I also hope to have shown that for readers who cannot check the translation against the original, the translation, quite simply, *is* the original. Rewriters and rewritings project images of the original work, author, literature, or culture that often impact many more readers than the original does. Rewritings of the kind analyzed in the past four chapters often conclusively shape the reception of a work, an author, a literature, or a society in a culture different from its culture of origin. In the next four chapters I turn to rewritings that shape the image and reception of a work, author, literature, society in their own culture.

9   Historiography

From bestseller to non-person: Willem Godschalk van Focquenbroch

The Dutch writer Willem Godschalk van Focquenbroch was born in Amsterdam in 1640 and probably died in 1670, on the West African Gold Coast where he had become treasurer of a settlement run by the Dutch East Indies Company after a somewhat less than successful career as a medical doctor in Amsterdam. He was a fairly prolific poet and playwright, as well as being the author who introduced the burlesque into Dutch literature, following the example of the French poet Scarron.

Focquenbroch was very popular for about a century after his death, during which time his works – the collected edition, which was by no means sold cheaply at the time – were reprinted eight times and his plays were produced on a regular basis. After about a century, both he and his work were more and more discredited in histories of Dutch literature, his books went out of print, his plays were no longer performed, and his name was all but forgotten, to be rediscovered only in the recent past.

In other words, generations of "specialists" in Dutch literature "edited out" Focquenbroch from their literature and culture. They did so because they had interiorized the discourse on literature dominant in their day, and Focquenbroch did not fit, or, in their opinion, could not be made to fit that discourse. In what follows, I shall attempt a survey of the main strategies used in this kind of "cultural editing," which is by no means restricted to Dutch literature but can easily be seen at work in other literatures as well.

"It is hard to understand," writes Bert Decorte in the introduction to his anthology of Focquenbroch's poetry, "how it could have been possible that nobody ever devoted himself to a thorough analysis of the life and work of this seventeenth-century author, which are both very remarkable, to put it mildly" (5). H. de Gooijer, the only nineteenth-century critic to rise to Focquenbroch's defense, took the matter philosophically: "Injustice is often done in the history of Dutch literature" (353).

The – often malign – neglect to which Focquenbroch has been subjected over the past three centuries is neither "unintelligible" nor due to some kind of impartial because impersonal, abstract justice or injustice. Indeed, the case of Willem Godschalk van Focquenbroch illustrates the extent to which histories of literature – and their spin-offs: reference works – are written subject to both ideological and poetological constraints.

Focquenbroch was immensely popular in the seventeenth century, but his pop-ularity was obviously not of the kind demanded by those "professionals" who shaped the dominant discourse on literature of his day. Focquenbroch's popular-ity was not of the right kind in the domain of poetics because the burlesque did not conform with the attempts of poets and critics to emulate the great examples of classical Antiquity, not least to demonstrate that the Dutch language, too, had "come of age" and could be a worthy vehicle for the various discourses to be used in the newly independent Republic of the United Provinces.

Nor was Focquenbroch's popularity of the right kind in terms of ideology, because neither his image as a writer of burlesque and satirical poems and plays nor the legend that had grown up around his person fitted the ideal image of seventeenth-century Amsterdam as the home of nation-builders, discoverers, seri-ous merchants, and poets with a message inspired either by the Bible or the ideals of Antiquity, and generally both.

Once a culture has arrived at a canonized image of its past, it tends to edit out those figures and features of that past that do not fit that image. An analysis of this process shows, once again, that the "intrinsic" value of a work of literature is by no means sufficient to ensure its survival. That survival is ensured at least to the same extent by rewritings. If a writer is no longer rewritten, his or her work will be forgotten.

The ideological reason for Focquenbroch's fall from popularity has perhaps been described most succinctly by Lode Baekelmans in the introduction to his anthology of Focquenbroch's poems: "The unsteadfast concept of decorum has made the poet van Focquenbroch almost forgotten" (9). J. C. Brandt Corstius, on the other hand, points out the poetological reason when he describes Focquen-broch as one of those poets who "were unable or unwilling to adapt to 'official' poetics" (123).

Ornee and Wijngaards add up the two factors in the equation when they state that "his burlesque style was obviously also a reaction against some puritanical currents in his time" (73), a point further elaborated on by Schenkeveld-van der Dussen: "Everything current opinion tends to value is negated by him, parodied or utterly ridiculed" (44–5). Focquenbroch did not, in other words, exactly appreci-ate the "decorum and the social arrogance" (van Heerikhuizen) of his time, nor did "the Renaissance ideals excite him the way they excited Hooft, Vondel, and Huygens – on the contrary" (Calis 26). Calis lists exactly the three writers who tried to rewrite Dutch literature in terms of the poetics of Antiquity: Hooft the poet, playwright, and historian, Vondel the playwright and poet, and Huygens the poet and playwright. It is significant, in this respect, that Huygens' only comedy, *Trijntje Cornelis,* contains burlesque language and situations that could have been taken straight from Focquenbroch. Why, then, was Focquenbroch ostracized and Huygens not? Because the whole of Focquenbroch's oeuvre was written under the sign of the burlesque, whereas Huygens, the diplomat, scientist, writer, and patri-cian, could afford to "descend" to that mode – once as a playwright, more often in his epigrams – since he would always safely "ascend" again to the discourse of decorum demanded by the age.

Before embarking on a closer analysis of the strategies used to edit Focquen-broch out of Dutch literary history, I must in all fairness point out that contemporary historiography is beginning to redress the balance. C. J. Kuik, for instance, writes in the introduction to his anthology of Focquenbroch's poems: "Midway through the seventeenth century and next to the universally recognized great authors, there lived a poet among us who has been forgotten because of his lack of seriousness, but whose ostensibly effortless parlando was of the kind our time seems to be willing to listen to once more" (11). Significantly, it is not the intrinsic value of Focquenbroch's work, which would have had to be timeless, if anything, that has been the only factor responsible for his rediscovery. The fact that the dominant poetics changed over the ages in such a way as to accommodate Focquenbroch's poetry once again is at least as important in this matter, combined with the further fact that the concept of "decorum" has also been significantly liberalized in the Netherlands since the end of World War Two.

Yet the more traditional position is also still with us. In the introduction to his anthology of the Dutch seventeenth-century sonnet, published in the same year as Kuik's anthology referred to above, Roose hastens to put the record "straight":

> once the reader has become familiar with Focquenbroch's ridiculing of the sonnet, he would be well advised to leaf again through this little book, which is devoted to the sonnet in one of its great periods, to check whether the genre to which the best of our poets devoted their powers is able to withstand this kind of caricature. In our opinion the experiment will yield positive results.
>
> (101)

Focquenbroch is, in other words, elevated from the position of "outcast" to that of "dissident." It is difficult to deny him all literary and cultural relevance, but he is still judged by comparison with "the best of our poets," whose poetics happen to be closer to the anthologist's taste than the poetics which guided Focquenbroch's composition. With the die loaded against him in such a way, Focquenbroch cannot but lose when it is cast.

Those attempting to "edit out" Focquenbroch were faced with one big problem, first stated by Witsen Geysbeek, and repeatedly since: "Reading a few pages of these so-called comic poems . . . would make anyone blessed with a certain taste and feeling of decorum vomit; nevertheless we are now looking at the third edition of the *excremental* smells of Focquenbroch's *Thalia,* which must certainly still have been read in 1766" (309). Fifty-nine years later, Worp is faced with the same problem; and he has managed to track down even more editions of Foc-quenbroch's works: "At least eight editions of the complete works have therefore been published within one century, an honor which was given to only a few of the poets of those days. It is not easy to explain Focquenbroch's success" (529). Consequently, Kobus and de Rivecourt, writing five years after Worp, do not even try. They simply state that "though some wit may shine through here and there, it is mostly cowardly and dirty, full of bad taste, coarsely burlesque" (542), meaning that Focquenbroch's idea of decorum does, indeed, not correspond to theirs. They then go on to state, without comment or even an attempt at transition of any kind: "and yet his poems were printed a number of times" (542).

Like all others in their camp, they cannot afford even to begin to think the obvious: Focquenbroch's poems were and remained so popular, in all probability, because they were what the majority of people living in Amsterdam's Golden Age deemed enjoyable in terms of both ideology and poetics, as is also evident from the forays both Hooft and Huygens periodically make into Focquenbroch's own domain. What has later been codified as the ideology and poetics of the "great poets" of the age – minus the burlesque and the scatological – was in all likelihood not dominant in that age but projected on it with hindsight by literary historians. Both that ideology and that poetics were projected on the age as part of an attempt to construct a "foundation myth" worthy of the new Republic. If Amsterdam was to be the new Rome, it could accommodate a Virgil, a Horace, a Seneca, a Tacitus; it did not need a Martial or a Juvenal just then.

Those who want to "edit out" Focquenbroch must, therefore, develop a double strategy. On the one hand, the reader must be told, as convincingly as possible, how "bad" Focquenbroch himself really was. On the other hand, his contemporaries must be absolved of any real "guilt" where his unfortunate, though happily short-lived popularity is concerned. They therefore need to be portrayed as probably somewhat less refined than the authors and readers of various rewritings, which would also explain why the "great poets" of the Golden Age sometimes bowed to their dubious taste. To sum up: even though the seventeenth century was indeed the Golden Age of Dutch culture, its denizens were prone to certain unfortunate lapses of taste which have since been remedied.

The second strategy first surfaces in Worp: "we are amazed, time and again, as we read, at what our forefathers were willing and able to listen to, and at the kind of puns they obviously appreciated" (503). Worp goes on to say, with an undertone of hidden regret:

> Our national character loved the coarse in comedy and poem, painting and drawing. The tone used at the weddings of our patrician families is too well known, as are the themes so masterfully treated by many of our painters; there is no need for me to go into it in detail.
>
> (530)

Kalff sympathizes, twenty-eight years later: "the old national character maintains itself in its commonsensical humor and its keen wit, but also in its coarseness that tended to mistake the dirty and the repulsive for the comic" (578). Both authors also (suspiciously?) echo each other in their evaluation of Focquenbroch's favorite mode: "Fortunately, however, his way of writing, the burlesque genre, has now completely gone out of fashion" (Worp 530). "Fortunately for the development of our people, the page was turned soon after" (Kalff 580).

As Baekelmans was the first to point out, both arguments can be used to cut both ways. If the seventeenth-century patricians tolerated coarseness in paintings and drawings and if those paintings and drawings are in museums nowadays, why then should the coarse literature they obviously also enjoyed be suppressed in anthologies and histories of literature? "The really rough, the coarsely sensual features of the paintings of his [Focquenbroch's] contemporaries and kindred spirits, such as Jan Steen, van Ostade, Joost van Craesbeek, Adriaan Brouwer, have not prevented them from being unconditionally praised through the centuries" (9), Baekelmans writes, and goes on to say that the burlesque, which is so obviously displayed in Dutch painting could not but surface in Dutch literature as well, mainly because the Dutch national character seems to have an affinity with it – or at least a certain kind of Dutch national character does, precisely the kind deemed "unseemly" by rewriters of literary history, though not by rewriters of art history. Focquenbroch, says Baekelmans, thereby offending the professionals of his time, was attracted to the burlesque because "for a Dutchman there was a deeper affinity with his own being" (17).

Baekelmans, whose anthology was published two years later than Kalff's history, could be dismissed as merely a lone dissenting voice at the time. But his point was fundamentally valid. The denizens of the glorious Dutch Golden Age were not as pure as they were often thought, or rather wished to be. To divert attention from these failings of the group as such, cultural editing singles out Focquenbroch as the black sheep, the writer given to exaggeration, who revels in the unfortunate vices of the age rather than trying to ennoble his contemporaries.

Since the same accusation could be leveled against canonized poets of the age, not only Hooft and Huygens, but also, and especially, Bredero, the strategy of character assassination becomes more and more unavoidable. Bredero at least can be said to have "repented" in religious terms, even though the poem usually interpreted as "proof" of his repentance turns out to have been a translation from the French, or to have been "ennobled" by his impossible love for a woman writer in the best tradition of medieval courtly love.

Focquenbroch's work is devoid of evidence of either. The strategy of character assassination therefore needs to be applied, in the most ruthless manner possible, to both the man and the poet. Before we analyze it in more detail we must keep two factors in mind. One is that "in spite of the increasing attention paid to Focquenbroch's life and work after World War Two, not much is known about his life to this day" (van Bork 206). Since not much is known, much can be inferred, or even invented with relative impunity. The other is that Focquenbroch "owes the reputation of libertine he has enjoyed for centuries to the backbiting of commentators who have been copying each other all too glibly" (Kuik 13). How glibly will become obvious in the following paragraphs.

Van der Aa writes in 1859: "he [Focquenbroch] met with little success because of his loose living, which is why he went to make his fortune on the coast of Guinea in 1666" (142). Worp's variation on this theme is published in 1881: "He did not meet with much success in his practice [as a medical doctor], probably at least in part because of his loose living. His funny poetry certainly did him no good either" (512). Worp then proceeds to embroider as follows: "the genre Focquenbroch wrote in was not fit to inspire confidence in patients, especially female patients" (512), and he ends up with the stock image of Focquenbroch based only on extrapolation from the written works. Worp, and others after him, take the persona Focquenbroch introduces in his poems for the person Focquenbroch himself. Moreover, neither he nor his successors make any allowances for the demands of genre: certain kinds of poetry require the persona to take a stance that is not exactly situated near the pinnacle of morality.

Whether or not Worp and his successors willfully identify the author with the work, Worp's summary of Focquenbroch's life was to go down in Dutch literary histories: "With an empty purse, a bad reputation, and a desperate love Focquenbroch left the fatherland in search for his fortune elsewhere" (512). In 1888 Frederiks and van den Branden inject a – probably involuntary – note of predestination by composing the following variation on Worp: "His readers probably never wondered about his departure to the coast of Guinea in 1666, where he was treasurer and died quickly, of course [sic]" (252). It is hard to avoid the impression that the Calvinist God personally punished Focquenbroch with early death.

In 1901 Everts writes about "the loose-living Willem Focquenbroch" (272). In 1920, Prinsen characterizes Focquenbroch as "a shady doctor, who ended up with a position on the Gold Coast" (294), contrasting him unfavorably with Pieter Bernagie, another "doctor who managed to maintain his dignity and later became a professor at the Athenaeum in Amsterdam" (294). The issue is not so much Focquenbroch's lack of financial success, but most definitely his lack of decorum, both in life and art, or rather in the life extrapolated from his art. In W. F. Hermans' words: "it is obvious by now why Focquenbroch haunts us as a shady doctor, but Vondel does not haunt us as a shady stocking merchant" (15) – even though Vondel's financial success was definitely not much greater than Focquenbroch's. The difference, of course, is that Vondel wrote the "right" literature, both for his own and later ages, while Focquenbroch did not. In 1924, Te Winkel writes that Focquenbroch "had made himself impossible as a doctor in Amsterdam (he had obtained his degree in 1662) because of his loose living" (278), and Ter Laan gives us the last "unredeemed" Focquenbroch as late as 1952: "He lived a life of loose morals while a student in Leiden and did not do much better as a doctor in Amsterdam" (158).

About twenty-five years later, we are introduced to the "new" Focquenbroch. While still not totally "redeemed" he is at least acceptable in the – more than slightly hackneyed – guise of the *poète maudit*. Since other literatures, the argument seems to go, do have them, why could not Dutch literature afford at least a few as long as it keeps them in a relatively marginal position. Rens still writes about "this Amsterdam man, who failed in his medical practice" (60), but adds in a tone that reveals understanding, though it most definitely does not condone:

> Focquenbroch suffers from life, which is too much for him. Nobody is more convinced of the vanity, senselessness, and cruelty of life than he is. With grim mockery and bitter cynicism, he demolishes the values, the opinions, the feelings, and the forms of his time, which are his as well. This pessimism of the *poète maudit* gives Focquenbroch modern features.
>
> (60)

In the same year, another literary historian describes "Doctor Focquenbroch, who kept himself busy in Amsterdam more with girls, drinking, and playing the flute than with practicing medicine" as "one of the most adventuresome and fascinating human types of our literature" (Dangez 118). It is significant, in this context, that Baekelmans, himself a writer, who did not always operate within the dominant ideology/poetics of his time, was the first to call Focquenbroch a *poète maudit* (9), sixty-four years before the dominant ideological and poetological parameters of their time had shifted far enough to allow both Rens and Dangez to use the same epithet in a discourse primarily aimed at a scholarly audience.

A comparison of the entries on Focquenbroch in the first and second editions of the *Moderne Encyclopedie der Wereldliteratuur* provides perhaps the most concise evidence of Focquenbroch's recent transformation. Minderaa, who wrote the entry for the first, 1965 edition, still says of Focquenbroch that "his practice did not flourish, probably because of his hobbies: smoking, drinking, sleeping around, playing the flute and the violin, conversing at great length, and writing poetry" (77). This sentence is omitted from the entry in the second, 1980 edition, written this time by "P. Minderaa and the Editors," which simply states that "although 'connoisseurs' in the seventeenth and eighteenth centuries were unable to appreciate his work, numerous reprints prove that the readers thought differently. The work is appreciated again in our century" (252).

Focquenbroch the poet is first attacked by Michiel de Swaen, in his *Nederduitsche Dichtkonde*. De Swaen numbers him among those who "humiliated the *Muses* down to the feet of the scum through the use of funny thoughts, and words" (281). He goes on to say that: "one can observe from the judgment of scholars what kind of respect these works of his deserve" (281). If we remind ourselves that the scholars de Swaen is referring to are the members of the Nil Volentibus Arduum society, whose predilection for French neoclassical poetics made it highly unlikely that they would treat Focquenbroch, or his French master Scarron, for that matter, with any respect, we can easily understand why de Swaen's remarks were fated to become a self-fulfilling prophecy.

In 1882, Witsen Geysbeek writes: "Focquenbroch passed in his time for a 'witty' and 'comic' poet, if one is allowed to call rude street language and indecent brothel mirth wit and comedy. We do not want to defile our paper by quoting examples of his grubby rhymes" (309). Thirty-seven years later, in 1859, van der Aa simply copies Witsen Geysbeek's words, defining Focquenbroch's poems as writings that "were considered witty and comical in his time, but which no longer deserve to be read or shown on the stage in our time because of the rude street language and the indecent brothel mirth that is found in them" (142). The exact same words surface again in Hofdijk, thirteen years later, in 1872, as part of his characterization of the "grubby Willem van Focquenbroch" (212). Thirty-seven years later, in 1909, Kalff writes that Focquenbroch is now barely known as "the poet of 'Diogenes the wise man/lived in a vat' " (580), a remark which surfaces again in almost exactly the same form in Ter Laan forty-three years later, in 1952: "These days we only know that drinking song of his: 'Diogenes the wise man/ lived in a vat' " (158).

Focquenbroch never had too many champions, especially not after his works went out of print. It was still relatively easy for his editor, Abraham Bogaert, to write: "Who does not burst out laughing when he puts his tones/To the wedding feast and sings the bride to bed/Who, joyous and awake/Awaits the groom who mollifies her with stories/And would rather have her moist field/Sown by him?" (3). In 1721, Pieter Langendijk is the last author and critic who is able to write about Focquenbroch in a tone that is neither vituperative nor apologetic. In his continuation of Focquenbroch's burlesque of the *Aeneid,* he pays the following homage to his predecessor:

Soon he also saw the African shores
Where Master Fok is buried
He took a small pipe between his teeth
And smoked respectfully
In honor of the great poet
As I today for that saint
That mind-refresher, bringer of joy
Light up a tasty pipe.
                              (470)

These are the last remarks on Focquenbroch in Dutch literary history that could be construed as friendly, even tender. In 1868, de Gooijer is already on the defensive when he asks why "what has been apologetically papered over in the case of others should be counted a deadly sin for Focquenbroch" (355). The others he mentions are Poot and, not surprisingly, Langendijk: "Did Poot not make himself guilty of hurting chaste ears?" and "was Langendijk always delicate?" (355). One could also add Bredero to de Gooijer's list, but the fact that he himself did not tends to underscore the strength of the taboo surrounding the canonized writers of the Dutch Golden Age.

De Gooijer also paves the way for the later image of Focquenbroch as *poète maudit* but without going as far as his fellow critics about a hundred years later: "True, he runs along the wrong road, but he does see the signposts that show him a better path" (360). We get Focquenbroch the potentially repentant sinner, whose sins can be explained though – again – not condoned by the fact that society "kept from him what he needed" (357). Unfortunately for Focquenbroch, the Golden Age already had its canonized repentant sinner, Bredero, and his inclusion in the canon also allowed the smuggling in of a modicum of the "low" and "coarse," but enough was, obviously, enough for most historians of Dutch literature. Focquenbroch found his potential niche already occupied, and it was impossible for him to dislodge Bredero whose "redemption" could at least be considered an "established" fact, whereas nobody knows, or is likely to know how Focquenbroch spent his last years. Bredero can be recuperated posthumously, Focquenbroch cannot.

By the year 1980, the Golden Age taboo had weakened enough for de Vooys and Stuiveling simply to link Focquenbroch's writings with "related work by Bredero or Starter," compared to which some of Focquenbroch's poems "can hold their own through directness of language and unadorned frankness" (71). Van Heerikhuizen recognizes Focquenbroch as a poet whose writings were inspired by a sense of protest against his time, but deplores "the direction in which this protest threatened to slide because it did not find a useful new ideal it could follow: the direction of tasteless coarseness that goes much farther in some of this poet's other verses" (83). It seems to have become acceptable not to be inspired by the ideals of the Golden Age as such, but burlesquing them is another matter – one that relegates you to the marginal position of the *poète maudit,* that convenient topos of literary history where Van Heerikhuizen meets with Rens and Dangez to create a Focquenbroch more acceptable to the literary establishment.

Two years later, though, Lodewick, Coenen, and Smulders take a step beyond that topos. Their description of Focquenbroch contains the following lines:

> Fortunately, the twentieth century displays a better understanding of this *independent spirit,* both for the simplicity and clarity of his language and for his poetry that is sometimes bitter, sometimes burlesque, but especially for his courage and honesty in seeing life and the world as they present themselves to him.
>
> (221)

Their verdict echoes that of two of their predecessors – W. F. Hermans, not very surprisingly: "And his original poetry was full of feeling, rich in atmosphere, technically very subtle and perfect, without rhetoric" (10), but also, surprisingly, Worp: "Moreover, our doctor's verses are not bad; he wrote easily and fluently and gave proof of great artistic talent in many a composite line" (580). Worp is prepared to compromise somewhat where poetics is concerned, but Focquenbroch remains damned because his ideology was at odds with the dominant ideology of his time.

Literary history, it would seem, is often written not from a timeless vantage point "above the fray"; rather, it often projects the "fray" of its own times back into the past, enlisting the support of those writers it canonizes for a certain ideology, a certain poetics, or both. A culture manipulates its past in the service of what dominant groups in that culture would like its present to be. The fact that our own present is kinder to Focquenbroch than the present of a hundred years ago just proves that poetics and ideologies do not last forever. There appears to be some kind of "historical moment" when the ideology and poetics of a time will shift far enough in a direction that will allow them to admit again those it cast out before.

Significantly, the anthologies of Focquenbroch's works published by Baekelmans and Hermans, both writers and therefore not "real" professional readers, were not able to bring about that shift. The groundwork for a new understanding of Focquenbroch seems rather to have been laid by a new generation of literary scholars who appear to have interiorized a culturally acceptable discourse on literature somewhat different from that interiorized by their predecessors.

10 Anthology
Anthologizing Africa

Publishers invest in anthologies, and publishers decide the number of pages they want to invest in. The "limitations of size" or "space" ritually lamented in almost all introductions to all anthologies are not a natural given. Rather, they reflect the anticipated demands of the market place. Howard Sergeant wrote in the introduction to his anthology, *African Voices*: "in presenting this anthology, however, I do not claim to have included the work of every poet of merit – indeed, for such a representation to have been at all possible, it would have been necessary to double the size of the volume" (xiii). Isidore Okpewho rather bluntly stated in the introduction to his *The Heritage of African Poetry*: "once again, I regret that I do not have space enough to represent as many poets, communities or pieces as might satisfy all and sundry" (34). Reed and Wake say essentially the same thing in the introduction to their *New Book of African Verse,* but in a more elegant manner: "in the interests of space we have also excluded the Malagasy poets we gave in 1964 adopting the stricter interpretation of the limits of African literature which is now usual" (1984: xii).

Publishers invest in a number of pages because they publish for a potential audience. Kgositsile has strong views on the composition of that audience: "who is the audience of the contemporary African writer? The bored Euro-American liberal literati searching for literary exotica in the African quarters of their empire? The African elite trained away from themselves in institutions of European design?" (xv). Not one of the anthologies discussed here has been published in Africa itself. All twelve were published in London, Harmondsworth, Bloomington, or New York.

A large part of the audience for African poetry today is White. Early attempts at canonizing African poets and projecting an image of African poetry have not been undertaken by African Blacks, but by European and American Whites. Since the audience for African poetry is relatively small, publishers will try to get as many potential readers as possible to buy the anthologies they publish. The result is competition, but also diversity of selection, at least since 1973, when new publishers try to break into the market by offering selections of new poets to their potential audience.

Publishers will be reluctant to invest too many pages in anthologies of African poetry, except perhaps if those anthologies can also be used as textbooks in schools (in Africa) and universities (in Africa and elsewhere). If an anthology is to function as a textbook, it had better not contain too much material that might be considered offensive by potential users. In 1964, Reed and Wake wrote in the preface of their anthology: "very little, for example, has come from the struggle in Southern and Central Africa" (4). Both Hughes and Moore and Beier, whose anthologies appeared one year earlier, include a fair number of anti-apartheid poems.

If publishers want to catch the attention of the potential White liberal audience, they should be ready with an anthology at a "historical moment" – when Africa is in the news outside Africa. It also helps to have the anthology either compiled or introduced by an established European or American (preferably Black) writer who can be shown to have a certain affinity with things African. African literature written in French was acceptable in Paris long before African literature written in English was deemed acceptable in London because "André Breton and Jean-Paul Sartre announced to the French the presence of the ambassadors of Négritude among them" (Chevrier 39). Breton had written a preface to Aimé Césaire's *Cahier d'un retour au pays natal* in 1947 and Sartre had written the preface to Léopold Sedar Senghor's *Anthologie de la nouvelle poésie nègre et malgache* in 1948. When Indiana University Press published its *Poems from Black Africa,* that anthology was compiled and introduced by Langston Hughes. Because the poetry of negritude had been accepted into the mainstream of French literature at least fifteen years earlier, Hughes devoted a fair number of pages to it, as did his immediate successors. The story of negritude was then considered a success story, eminently suitable for emulation by African poets writing in English.

The simple availability of texts also constitutes a constraint under which anthologists of African poetry have to operate. Only five of the anthologies mentioned here include oral poetry, ancient or modern. Within the corpus of oral poetry made available in English by these five anthologies, Yoruba claims twenty-seven poems, Ewe is a distant second with eight, followed closely by Akan with seven. Swahili follows with six poems, Amhara and Zulu each reach a total of four, and no other African language is represented with more than three. This state of affairs does not reflect the overwhelming superiority of Yoruba oral poetry, but merely the fact that it has been studied and translated for a longer time, and by more people. Similarly, the relative dominance of Nigerian poets in Moore and Beier's 1984 edition can be accurately explained by the fact that Nigeria "does after all contain almost half the continent's black population" (22).

Translations from African literature written in French were usually available for inclusion in anthologies of African poetry published in English, but the same cannot be said for translations from the Portuguese. These began to surface on a larger scale only when the anti-colonial struggle in Angola and Mozambique began to be mentioned in White liberal newspapers and on the evening news with some regularity.

The poetics the anthologists subscribe to also helps shape the anthology. In 1963, for instance, Moore and Beier decided to include only "modern" poetry from Africa in their anthology. They defined "modern" as "a matter of the poets' awareness of the modern idiom in European and American poetry. It is this awareness that enables them to use their respective languages without distracting archaism and in a way that appeals instantly to the contemporary ear" (30). In the 1984 edition "modern" has simply come to mean "a major concern with craft" (23), but it is still upheld as a criterion for selection, even though the 1984 selection is more heavily weighted toward the political, as a counterpart maybe also to Reed and Wake who stated in the preface to their 1984 edition: "our taste has led us more towards poems of experience and observation than to those of philosophical consideration and political declaration, more towards a poetry of direct utterance than of allusion and elaboration" (xii).

Once a certain degree of early canonization has been attained in African poetry, roughly around 1970, new anthologies can accept that emerging canon, try to subvert it, or try to enlarge it. The three anthologies published in 1973 by Allen, Kgositsile, and Sergeant engage in conscious canon building, as does Okpewho's anthology published in 1985. Anthologies published after 1974, on the other hand, tend to reinforce the pre-existing canon. While they introduce new poets, they do not significantly expand either the thematic or the poetological range already established.

Okpewho's title *The Heritage of African Poetry* suggests that he is consciously building a heritage which will embrace both the present and the past, and this necessarily implies a revalorization of oral poetry. Accordingly, Okpewho states the need "to give the oral traditional poetry of Africa its deserved place both in the literary curriculum and in our general understanding of what poetry tries to do" (3). Kgositsile and Sergeant, on the other hand, both define themselves as anti-canonical, or as the builders of the "real" canon. Kgositsile dedicates his anthology to the memory of Langston Hughes and Chris Okigbo, among others, laying claim to the mantle of both the first anthologist of African poetry in English and the man considered by many to have been Africa's most important poet. Armed with these credentials Kgositsile states that poetry "if it is authentic, as anything else expressive of a people's spirit, is always social" (xv), announcing the poetics underlying his anthology. Sergeant does not have a "real" canon ready to take the place of the existing one. He simply believes that canon formation should never come to a closure. He therefore states "I have deliberately given more space to new and little-known poets" (xv).

A first image of African poetry is projected in the three anthologies published in 1963 and 1964. A second, anti-canonical wave of three anthologies is published in 1973, and the situation remains relatively stable from then on. Langston Hughes's anthology *Poems from Black Africa* justifies its existence by stating that it is time to try to understand Africa, not only because its future "is coming more and more into the control of the peoples of Africa themselves" (11), but also because "art and life have not yet parted company in Africa." Hughes obviously refers to the idealized Africa then so much in evidence in the poetry of negritude he daringly extends to cover English-speaking Africa as well, albeit on the flimsiest of grounds: "the best poetry of both French and English expression bears the stamp of the African personality, and most of its emotional aura might be included with the term *négritude*" (13). This is not a statement of fact, but of strategy: since the African poets writing in French have achieved success in France with negritude, African poets writing in English should emulate them.

In his selections, Hughes tries to balance a strategy of analogy with one of cautious exoticism. Since he is introducing new poets and new themes, the best way to help readers "place" the new is to tell them it is "like" something they already know. Hughes therefore mentions in his introduction that "the French African poets, and particularly Senghor, tend toward creating Whitmanesque catalogues" (12). One of his selections is an African "Nativity": "Within a native hut, ere stirred the dawn/Unto the Pure One was an Infant born/Wrapped in blue lappah that His mother dyed/Laid on His father's home-tanned deerskin hide" (76). Yet the anthology also includes Wole Soyinka's "Abiku," a poem about children, but with a Yoruba twist. Hughes states in his headnote to the poem that Abiku "is the Yoruba myth of infant mortality, meaning literally 'born to die.' It is believed that the dead child returns to plague the mother" (103). He then proceeds to print the poem in full, even though it represents a far cry from the Romantic idealization of childhood. Hughes also includes a selection from the oral poetry then available to him, but his headnotes betray a certain ignorance of African reality, listing both "Bantu" and "Johannesburg" as "languages."

Hughes's anthology already contains all the themes that will surface again in all subsequent anthologies, even if they are not always given the same space. Some themes are traditional in African poetry: love, including the relationship to the woman as mother, lover, mythical incarnation of a country, or even of the whole continent; death; continuity and change; the role of the poet; descriptions of the environment. Other themes are more topical: colonialism, apartheid, the African between two cultures, rewritings of African history. Hughes links the traditional and the topical by emphasizing their natural meeting point: negritude.

Hughes's anthology also already contains a core of poets who will find their way into all subsequent anthologies: David Rubadiri, Kwesi Brew, Gabriel Okara, John Pepper Clark, Christopher Okigbo, Wole Soyinka, Chicaya U Tam'si, Léopold Sedar Senghor, and David Diop. He also includes the Malagasy poets Rabéarivelo and Ranaivo who will be subtly edged out of subsequent anthologies "for lack of space."

Gerald Moore and Ulli Beier do not include oral poetry in their 185-page *Modern Poetry from Africa* published in the same year because their selection is primarily based on poetics. What they select must be modern, i.e. it must "represent a fresh exploration of language" (20). For this reason, they exclude the so-called "pioneer poets" belonging to the very first generation of Africans to write in English who are afflicted "with a total lack of style" (20). In the same year in which Hughes declares all African poetry to be written under the sign of negritude, Moore and Beier suggest that "the wellspring of Négritude is running dry" (23), and that the climate of Ibadan, the university city of Nigeria where many of the Nigerian poets of the first generation received their higher education – from Moore and Beier, among others – is more conducive to the development of African poetry than that of pre-war Paris, because the young poets who studied at Ibadan "were able to acquire a literary culture without suffering the sense of alienation and exile which afflicted the black writers gathered in Paris twenty and thirty years ago" (20).

Thematically Moore and Beier's anthology is not different from Hughes's, probably because there is a hard core of traditional African subjects for poetry that runs through all anthologies, possibly even unbeknownst to anthologizers, until it surfaces in the themes that orchestrate the composition of Soyinka's 1975 anthology and that are reaffirmed by Okpewho's anthology ten years later. Moore and Beier introduce one more traditional African type of poetry: the reflective, philosophical poem. They also introduce two more topical themes: individualism and African politics. The latter is already beginning to be treated in the satirical mode. Moore and Beier give more space to poems dealing with the struggle against (as opposed to the triumph over) colonialism, particularly in the translations from the Portuguese included in their selection. Since their selection is guided primarily by poetics, it stands to reason that they also give more space to poems emphasizing the role of the poet in society, just as they give more scope to poets most conscious of their craft: Senghor goes from five poems in Hughes to thirteen in Moore and Beier, Okigbo from one to seven, Soyinka from one to eight, Clark from two to nine. The new poets introduced by Moore and Beier join the core group that will be found in most subsequent anthologies. They are Lenrie Peters, Kofi Awoonor, Michael Echeruo, Mazisi Kunene, Agostinho Neto, and Birago Diop.

James Reed and Clive Wake published their 119-page anthology, *A Book of African Verse,* in 1964. They did not introduce any new themes, but dropped the theme of apartheid. The only Southern African poem they include is an extract (19 pages) from a long narrative poem originally written in Xhosa on the life of the Xhosa maiden Thuthula. In the second edition, published twenty years later, Reed and Wake include names belonging to "the remarkable constellation of poets which arose" in South Africa (xii), but not without adding that "James Jolobe's long narrative poem *Thuthula*" will "perhaps" be "particularly" (xii) missed among the 1964 selections they had to omit. Compared to Hughes and to Moore and Beier, Reed and Wake significantly increased the number of poems by two Malagasy poets, Rabéarivelo and Ranaivo, only to omit them altogether in the 1984 edition. None of the new poets introduced by Reed and Wake in 1964 have survived in subsequent anthologies.

Together with Moore and Beier's anthology (enlarged in 1968), Reed and Wake's was the most widely distributed, and therefore potentially most influential anthology of African poetry. It was distributed in its 1964 form for twenty years, during which it gradually lost touch with developments in Africa itself. It is a sobering thought indeed that the reader who turns to Reed and Wake after the 1976 Soweto riots to find out about South African poetry will be given only *Thuthula,* to read. There is no significant thematic difference between the 1963 Moore and Beier and its 1968 successor, but the new Moore and Beier introduced the third wave of poets who also found their way into the core group: Mbella Sonne Dipoko, Dennis Brutus, Keorapetse Kgositsile, and Okot p'Bitek.

In terms of poetics, the anthologies published between 1963 and 1968 span a wide spectrum indeed. On the one hand there are the "pioneer poets" who "seem not only parochial, but strangely archaic with stanzas and diction derived from hymns or Victorian ballads" (Moore and Beier 1984: 23). On the other hand there are the Ibadan poets of the early sixties whose poetry "often suffers from an over-dose of Pound, Hopkins and Eliot" (Moore and Beier 1984: 23). In both cases, the poets are obviously influenced by the mode that was dominant in English-language poetry during their formative years. The difference is that one mode finds favor with the poetics espoused by Moore and Beier while the other does not.

Reed and Wake point out obvious influences on some of their selections: *Thuthula* "is closely modeled on the narrative blank verse of . . . Alfred, Lord Tennyson" (1964: 3). Gabriel Okara "writes in a way which suggests he has been deeply influenced by Dylan Thomas" (3), while "David Rubadiri's poem *Stanley Meets Mutesa* has been influenced by T. S. Eliot's *The Journey of the Magi*" (3). Reed and Wake's poetics are more catholic than Moore and Beier's, but what happened in both generations is obviously the same: the budding poets were confronted with models that were "in" at their time and began to imitate them, as budding poets do everywhere. One can extend the game and point out that Rubadiri's "The Tide that from the West washes Africa to the Bone," anthologized in Sergeant, is tributary to Dylan Thomas's "The force that through the green fuse drives the flower," while Eliot and Dylan Thomas have both influenced Arthur Nortje's "London Impressions II," anthologized in Wole Soyinka's *Poems of Black Africa*. Finally, Hopkins is a pervasive influence on Dennis Brutus's sonnet "At a Funeral," anthologized in Moore and Beier's 1968 edition. If anthologists select on the basis of a poetics, they will exclude what cannot be reduced to that poetics; they will not exclude the same poets or poems if they select on a basis other than that of a poetics.

The year 1973 witnesses the publication of three more or less "anti-canonical" anthologies of African poetry. Samuel Allen's 205-page *Poems from Africa* omits translations from the Portuguese but includes oral poetry because that poetry "reflects a vigorous and purposeful life with a full measure of satisfaction, as well as sorrow, within a framework of meaning and fulfillment" (4). The image of Africa contained in oral poetry is explicitly designed to counteract the image that "has for so long been dominated by the popular distortions of an Edgar Rice Burroughs, a Vachel Lindsay or a mindless cartoon television industry" (1). Allen's anthology thus projects its own image of Africa in an attempt to correct current clichés.

The theme of African politics is treated with more sadness and bitterness than before and the resulting disillusionment with public affairs leads to increased concentration on the self: "the Nigerian poets, particularly, turned from public themes to individual concerns" (6). The theme of apartheid is represented in Allen's anthology, but there is a noticeable discrepancy between the way he deals with it in his introduction as opposed to the actual selections he includes. The introduction states: "in the modern poetry of South Africa, there is one major theme – the continued suffering of an oppressed people. The expression of pain and outrage in this poetry is similar to that of the earlier poetry of négritude in the period before African nations began to gain freedom" (11). The actual selections consist of extracts from three narrative poems, set well in the past, one meditation on the ocean, another on parting, and four poems actually dealing with apartheid itself, one a Zulu poem, one by Kunene, and two by Brutus. Nortje and Kgositsile, who had already emerged by then, are not included.

Howard Sergeant does not include French-speaking poets in his 137-page *African Voices,* an anthology that represents a deliberate attempt to "give more space to new and little-known poets" (xiv). Yet of the many poets Sergeant introduces, only Jared Angira, Amin Kassam, and John/Atukwei Okai will find their way into most subsequent anthologies. Sergeant gives less space to the – by then fading – struggle against colonialism than to African politics, particularly the Biafran War. The theme of individualism gains more ground and poems on themes not specifically African but related to world politics, such as the 1967 Arab–Israeli War, are included. Most space is devoted to poems describing man's environment, whether nature or the city. The treatment of the theme of apartheid goes quite consciously against the grain as evidenced by selections such as Richard Rive's "Where the Rainbow ends," one of the most conciliatory poems on the subject ever written by a Black poet.

In the introduction to his 173-page *The Word is Here,* Keorapetse Kgositsile states: "poetry, as any other art form, as social comment, serves an educational purpose. In our time, then, the African poet is either a tool of oppression or seeks to be an agent of liberation" (xvi). By polarizing the situation from the very beginning, Kgositsile tries to justify his attempt to leave out one pole altogether. The poets gathered in his anthology are all "agents of liberation" but of all the poets he introduces only one, Ama Ata Aidoo, who has been represented in more than one subsequent anthology. Because of his political stance Kgositsile includes the more militant negritude poets U'Tamsi and David Diop, but not Senghor. He also includes militant poets from North Africa not normally considered to fall within "the stricter interpretation of the limits of African literature" (Reed and Wake 1984: xii). Yet he omits Portuguese-speaking poets altogether, with the exception of Agostinho Neto, even though their poetry would perfectly fit its ideological stance. In this, he is probably the victim of the availability constraint.

Predictably, Kgositsile devotes a fair number of poems to African politics. The Biafran War looms large as the expression of the supreme disillusionment. History is rewritten, but this time also from a Black woman's point of view in Stella Ngatho's "The Kraal," a poem that strongly conveys the impression that Africa's past may have been somewhat less than glorious for Africa's women, no matter to what extent the male poets of negritude have idealized it. Apartheid also gets a fair number of poems. Dennis Brutus concentrates on the dehumanizing aspects of petty apartheid but he is also, somewhat less predictably, represented with the fourteenth "Letter to Martha" that contains the lines: "How fortunate we were/not to have been exposed/to rhetoric/it would have falsified/a simple experience" (89), an eloquent and studied contrast to the fierce rhetoric of both the North African poets and the poets of negritude. The theme of colonialism is represented by poems concerning the (im)possibility of assimilation.

In 1975, Wole Soyinka published his *Poems of Black Africa,* an obvious attempt at a "definitive" anthology. Soyinka, perhaps then already the most prominent African writer, was called upon to mediate between the Black experience and the

"Euro-American liberal literati" by the London publishers Secker and Warburg, who had, until then, left African poetry to Penguin, Longman, and, especially, Heinemann. Soyinka's anthology includes both the 1963–8 poets and a number of the 1973 poets. It also introduces Oswald Mtshali, Odia Ofeimun, and Taban Lo Lyiong whose work appears in subsequent anthologies.

Selections from the work of the poets represented are more generous than in other anthologies. Soyinka includes French-, English-, and Portuguese-speaking poets as well as oral poetry. The format of the anthology is such that it can be both read for pleasure and used in teaching, especially after its reissue as a paperback in the Heinemann African Writers Series, which marked the end of Secker and Warburg's brief foray into the African poetry market. The publisher invested a generous number of pages, 378, by far the largest number invested in any anthology under discussion here. Soyinka's anthology, then, is one of consolidation. All the well-known names are here, often with their "signature poems" that have become familiar from previous anthologies, and all the themes included from Hughes onwards are represented, including those no longer considered topical in some of the anthologies published in 1973.

The space Soyinka devotes to the various themes reflects the changes in their relative importance since Hughes first introduced them in 1963. Soyinka introduces thirteen poems that deal with the theme of the African torn between two cultures; sixteen poems are devoted to the theme of continuity; thirty-three poems deal with descriptions of the environment; twenty poems describe the struggle against colonialism; sixteen are devoted to apartheid; thirty to love and woman; ten to death; and twelve to the role of the poet – a remarkable homage to the thematic continuity of African poetry. Two other themes represented in Soyinka's anthology were not introduced by Hughes, but by Moore and Beier, also in 1963. Soyinka devotes thirty poems to African politics, especially the Biafran War, and eight poems to the development and analysis of the self. It is not too difficult, of course, to explain the continuity exhibited by Soyinka's anthology by referring to the continuity inherent in postcolonial developments all over Africa, and by the fact that most of the themes are those of traditional African poetry anyway.

K. E. Senanu and T. Vincent's 224-page *A Selection of African Poetry* is designed for use in the classroom. Their introduction manages to overlook the existence of Soyinka's anthology, probably in the interest of marketability. They deplore the absence "of an anthology that cannot only be used as an introduction to poetry in Africa but aims to display the varied beauty of African poetry" (1), which is exactly what Soyinka's anthology had done. Because the anthology is intended specifically for the classroom, poets considered "too difficult," like Christopher Okigbo, are left out.

Senanu and Vincent accept the canon at face value: "beginning with samples of traditional poetry followed by a selection from older poets like Léopold Senghor and Birago Diop, we provide a historical perspective" (2). The pioneers of negritude have become "classics" to the same extent as oral poetry, but they are treated in a different way. Senghor's work is subjected to a less than enthusiastic reappraisal: many of his poems "are emotional and oversentimental, especially the nostalgic reminiscences" (23). Senghor is beginning to move toward the same twilight zone to which Moore and Beier banished the work of the English-speaking pioneer poets, and for the same reason: his poetics no longer coincide with the dominant poetics of the day. Oral poetry, on the other hand, is staunchly defended, mainly because Africa is now seen to need a "classical" poetry to back up its established modernity. Furthermore, oral poetry, once dismissed by White missionaries as "not literature," is now considered a "constant reminder of the true origins of a form generally regarded as the highest type of artistic expression" (9). The African, it would appear, is closer to the wellsprings of poetry as such than the White man who has lost all contact with oral poetry as a living tradition.

By 1980, the study of African poetry had become institutionalized in Africa and, to a certain extent, also in Europe and North America. Once institutionalized, it found itself able to command a relatively stable market, and publishers were ready to invest more paper in updating the two most popular early anthologies. Reed and Wake brought out *A New Book of African Verse* in 1984, and in the same year Moore and Beier published the third edition of their anthology under a new title: *Modern African Poetry.* Since they had not revised their anthology since 1964, Reed and Wake seized this opportunity to omit thirty-three poems and to add seventy-nine. They continued the trend toward universalization of African poetry, first anthologized in Sergeant and still apologized for in Senanu and Vincent. Reed and Wake simply include John Pepper Clark's "Incident at the Police Station, Warri" with its subtitle "After *The Flagellation of Jesus* by Piero della Francesca" without any apology. Admittedly, Warri is a Nigerian town, but the reference to Renaissance Europe universalizes the poem's subject matter. In the case of negritude, the trend toward revisionism continues. Lenrie Peters scathingly reduces the African "self" extolled by Senghor to "chocolate icing and mascara 'selves' " (74). African politics are approached with a growing feeling of resignation, and apartheid, which does not seem to have crumbled under the combined weight of all the poems written against it, now inspires somewhat of a millenarian attitude, as in Nortje's poem "Native Letter" that expresses the hope that the "cycles of history" will outnumber "the guns of supremacy" (55).

Moore and Beier revise less extensively than Reed and Wake but their stance has become more avowedly political, if notably less optimistic between 1968 and 1984. Their introduction states: "loss of liberty, of life, of the hopes and companions of one's youth, runs through the poetry of this selection like a flood" (19). They appear to be especially taken with the Angolan struggle against colonialism, most probably because a situation in which "poetry and resistance went hand in hand, many poets becoming fighters and many fighters turning to poetry" (21) allows them silently to widen the selection criteria, based exclusively on poetics, that they used in earlier editions of their anthology. Consequently, the section on Angola is much enlarged in the 1984 edition and more translations from the Portuguese are included in the anthology as a whole. African politics is treated with resignation, but new developments appear. There is the desire for a new departure, away from the old themes and the old clichés, especially the old clichés about Blacks, the myths that "make of us naiveté" as Sepamla puts it in his poem "On

Judgment Day" (265). There is also, one is tempted to add "finally," the desire to change the preconditions of poetic discourse altogether, to escape "The Strangle-hold of English Lit.," to quote the title of an Mtshali poem anthologized by Moore and Beier in their 1984 edition (139).

Published in 1985, Isidore Okpewho's *The Heritage of African Poetry* is perhaps the most conscious effort at canon building to date. It works back from the (estab-lished) present to the past, trying to link both by means of a thematic approach. Like Senanu and Vincent, whose anthology was also published by Longman, Okpewho does not refer to Soyinka's thematic anthology first published by Secker and Warburg and then reissued by Heinemann. About half the poems included in Okpewho's *Heritage* belong to the oral tradition – considerably more than ever before. The other half represents the familiar names as well as the familiar themes most of which did, of course, belong to the oral tradition all along.

Since Okpewho's anthology represents African poetry as institutionalized for use in African schools and African and non-African universities alike, it contains no thematic or poetological surprises and it introduces no new names. The canon has not only been established; it has also been extended back in time. There will be room for others to join, but the battles over the criteria for inclusion or exclu-sion need not be fought all over again. By contrast the 1984 anthologies intro-duced such bitter new talent as Sid Cheney-Coker, Sipho Sepamla, Mongane Wally Serote, and Jack Mapenje. They also introduced English poems written in both the surrealist and the expressionist vein, as well as Serote's "performance poetry" which, in different circumstances, links up with other kinds of "live readings" of poetry practiced on other continents. They even introduce self-parody: since Afri-can poetry has become established, and since its oral ancestry is acknowledged, it has become admissible to parody oral literature and to write "mock orals" like Kofi Anyiodoho's (anthologized in Moore and Beier 1984: 103) in which ancestral gods speak of thieving politicians in a strange mixture of mythological register and street slang.

Maybe the distance between Hughes and 1984 can best be measured by means of a comparison between Hughes's African "Nativity" quoted above, with its "charm-ing" adaptation by one of the "pioneer" poets of the Christmas story to "native" conditions, and Mtshali's use of the Easter story as an allegory for the powers that be in South Africa in "Ride upon the Death Chariot" anthologized in Moore and Beier. The first stanza of that poem reads: "They rode upon/the death chariot/to their Golgotha/three vagrants/whose papers to be in Caesar's empire/were not in order" (272). The African "Nativity" is written in the poetics of imported dis-course. Mtshali's poem is one of an increasing number of attempts by Black poets to make use of White symbols, as they make use of White forms in a discourse increasingly their own.

11 Criticism

Beyond her gender: Madame de Staël

When Madame de Staël died in Paris in 1817, she was known all over Europe as a great writer, a brilliant mind, an important political figure who had opposed Napoleon during much of his rule, an exceedingly wealthy lady, and a woman who had had affairs with some of the most important men of her time, and many of lesser importance besides. After her death her family wanted her remembered on all counts listed above, except the last one. Since the family had also inherited both her wealth and her private papers, it could make use of both to further its purposes. In the words of one of the critics considered here, Françoise d'Eaubonne, the family wanted to "substitute for the real person a legendary figure as likely and as exact as those of the saints in official hagiography" (260). Since the family was rich and powerful enough to act as its own patron, it almost completely succeeded in its aim for a number of years. It also established the parameters of critical discourse on Madame de Staël down to the present.

In this chapter, I propose to analyze the strategies employed by critics writing on Madame de Staël. I have deliberately adopted the stance of the non-professional reader of literature who might become interested in Madame de Staël and might, therefore, want to gather some information about her. I have made a choice from critical works published – in France only, for reasons that will become apparent below – between 1820 and 1987, simply by picking books published a sufficient number of years apart to warrant the assumption that they might be relatively different from each other. Like the non-professional reader, I have not necessarily focused on the "best" or "most acclaimed" works on Madame de Staël, but on the works he or she is likely to discover in libraries of a certain size, and read in no particular predetermined order.

The year 1820 witnessed the publication of both the first "hagiography" of Madame de Staël, written by her cousin, Albertine Necker de Saussure, as "Requested by the children of Madame de Staël" (1), and Victor Cousin d'Avalon's somewhat less enthusiastic appraisal of the recently deceased. Necker de Saussure makes her first strategic move on page 2 of her book by saying of Madame de Staël: "Nothing that she has produced is comparable to herself" (2). By downgrading the published work in favor of the personality of the writer, Necker de Saussure shifts the discourse to a level where it can be more easily controlled by those who hold the key to that personality: the personal archives that give them the power to rewrite Madame de Staël's personal life as they see fit. To this day most critical works published on Madame de Staël focus on her personality rather than her work. Even where they – sometimes vehemently – disagree with Necker de Saussure, they do not attempt to shift the parameters of the discourse established by her.

Madame de Staël's writings are downgraded not once, but twice. Not only is her work represented as inferior to her personality, but Necker de Saussure goes on to suggest that Madame de Staël never really intended to produce "art" as such: "in writing she always sought rather to express what passed in her own mind than to produce a work of art" (7). Accordingly, her work should be read mainly as an indicator of the "traces of her character" (6) that should be the real object of criticism. To this day, with the exception of one or two studies published in the very recent past, all criticism of Madame de Staël has remained solidly biographical. Even critics who lament this fact, such as Marie-Louise Pailleron, who rightly remarks that: "it remains a fact that neither her partisans nor her detractors have taken the trouble of reading her work – much more extraordinary, by the way, than her person" (43), fail to shift the parameters of critical discourse first established in 1820.

The only reference Joseph Turquan, for instance, makes to the actual writings of Madame de Staël is the following: "Madame de Staël tried to console herself for her political failures by producing literature" (138). The title of Turquan's book, with its reference to Madame de Staël's "amorous" and "worldly," as well as her "political," life is a good indication of the excesses to which the biographical approach could, and did, lead. A fair number of remarks made in a fair number of books on Madame de Staël fail to rise above the level of malicious gossip. The only way critics appear to be able to draw attention to the actual writings of Madame de Staël within the established parameters is by quoting from them at some – sometimes inordinate – length. To quote André Larg: "One would have to quote everything" (54). But the quotations are mostly either left to stand on their own, or made explicit only to shore up some biographical point the authors wish to make.

Necker de Saussure does refer to Madame de Staël's verbal artistry, but only to that part of it which was never actually written down, and can therefore not be commented on except in – usually glowing – general terms: her conversation. We are told that "The succession of thoughts is too rapid and continual in Madame de Staël to allow ordinary minds to keep pace with it" (Necker de Saussure 200). Maria Child echoes Necker de Saussure when she writes that "we cannot realize the vividness of her fame, like those who saw her genius flashing and sparkling in quick collision with kindred minds" (100). Even those critics whose attitude toward Madame de Staël is rather negative have to acknowledge her conversational skills – ironically on the basis of the information imparted in the "hagiographies" written by some of their predecessors – but they manage to twist it to their purpose. Joseph Turquan writes: "Like all women, Madame de Staël received at birth a gift of speech superior to that allotted to men" (176). The conversationalist as chatterbox resurfaces in Larg: "In the month of June, between two conversations, as it were, Madame de Staël gave birth to a daughter, Albertine" (226), and in d'Eaubonne, squarely on the "level" of gossip: "Was she even silent while making love? Posterity did not leave us anything concerning this interesting detail" (45).

Once she has firmly established the parameters of critical discourse about Madame de Staël, Albertine Necker de Saussure "has made of her the prototype of genius, talent and virtue" (Cousin d'Avalon 2). Necker de Saussure understandably uses a different level of diction. For her Madame de Staël "still animates it [the French nation] with hope, and points out to it, with her celestial palm-branch, the path of true glory and sage liberty" (16). Yet, though she may be canonized as a saint in the traditional fashion, Madame de Staël, who could be portrayed as a "martyr" under Napoleon, certainly could never be portrayed as a "virgin" in the canonical sense. Her affairs were too numerous and too well known for that. She was, in Turquan's words: "not a woman to be shocked by her own immorality" (16). Necker de Saussure counters with the strategy of selective memory. She does not admit to any affairs, even to the point of referring to Benjamin Constant, Madame de Staël's lover for fourteen years, as "a writer now highly celebrated, Mr. Benjamin Constant" (114) – and there an end. Necker de Saussure brings selective memory to play in the description of Madame de Staël's unhappy first marriage to the Baron de Staël, Swedish ambassador to the court of Louis XVI: "At present, when I tax my memory, I would endeavour to recollect particulars of Baron de Staël, but I scarcely knew him" (236).

The strategy of selective memory is supplemented by that of apology. Madame de Staël was, after all, only human, and may therefore have erred somewhat in that most human of emotions: love. Without admitting to any of Madame de Staël's affairs, Necker de Saussure apologizes for her second marriage, to a person Larg describes as: "a young phthisic invalid, without reason or culture, obsessed by a fixed idea – an absurd union with disastrous consequences" (166). Necker de Saussure does not discuss the actual merits or demerits of the groom, but berates Madame de Staël for having kept the marriage a secret, while at the same time marshaling attenuating circumstances in her defense:

> She would have done better, no doubt, had she avowed this marriage; but a degree of timidity, from which the sort of courage she possessed did not emancipate her, and her attachment to the name she had rendered illustrious . . . restrained her.
>
> (270)

A similar note of apology creeps into Maria Child's description of Madame de Staël's "friendships": "The impetuosity of an unsatisfied spirit gave a singular degree of vehemence to all her attachments; her gratitude and friendship took the coloring of ardent love" (29) – but only to the outside observer who did not "really" know the "real" Madame de Staël.

The strategy of apology makes avid use of arguments of a psychological nature that range from pre-Freudian prejudices linked with a certain idea of woman over trivializations of Freudian concepts to Lacanian reinterpretations of those concepts. Before Freud, Maurice Souriau writes: "With Madame de Staël, when you don't understand, look for a man" (81). D'Eaubonne uses Freudian cliché to explain Madame de Staël's taste for affairs: "Germaine will for ever suffer from what she, together with those who judge her, takes for 'ugliness'; it is in this anguish of humiliation that she will find the need for amorous adventures, diverse, frequent and repeated, much more so than in the ardor of her nature" (48). In other words: if Madame de Staël had been prettier, she would not have had any affairs, or certainly not as many. Long after Freud, Diesbach writes that Madame de Staël "does not hide her need to have a strong man she can dominate" (102), and since she never found one she had no alternative but to continue her quest. Turquan is of the opposite persuasion: "A man of iron would have been needed to make love spring forth in her" (44). He even has the right candidate in mind: "Mirabeau would have been the male for this female" (44). Larg points out the "femininity" in the character of three of Madame de Staël's lovers (Narbonne, Constant, Rocca) and states unequivocally: "It was this femininity which brought them together in the first instance" (133). Vallois has recourse to another cliché: Madame de Staël suffered from "a fundamental lack, that of a lover identical to her father" (9). The father himself is given a little Lacanian twist when the reader's attention is drawn to "The intimate relationship which links the paternal figure with tragic law" (Vallois 118). It is remarkable that each of the critics mentioned here claims to have found the key to Madame de Staël's personality, that each thinks there can only be one key, and that each opts for a different key, probably also because the repertoire of cliché psychology tends to be somewhat limited.

But that repertoire is easily supplemented by another repertoire of clichés that is much older and does not claim any scientific status. It should not be forgotten, after all, that Madame de Staël was a woman, and that women have been caricatured by men over the centuries. Pailleron resorts to a judicious mixture of psychological and "woman" clichés when she explains Madame de Staël's adversarial relationship with Napoleon Bonaparte as follows: "this antipathy was the reverse of a greater love; that love repulsed changed into a hatred more apparent than real: a woman's heart is full of weakness" (115).

Souriau sounds the familiar patronizing note in his analysis of Madame de Staël's ethical concepts: "she contradicts herself, and pretends for the rest that she does not, which is very feminine, and even rather human" (23), thus firmly establishing Madame de Staël as a member of a subspecies of the human race – women – and as someone who was out of her depth in a world that was not her own and should never have ventured outside the world Turquan delimits for her. He deplores the fact that Madame de Staël, like many other women

> greedy for glory, pleasure and violent sensations, only think of their success. They would not deign to lower themselves to the sweet role of a spouse who makes the happiness of her husband; of a mother who guides her children's education in the right direction; of a homemaker who makes her home a pleasant place because of her amiability. And yet that is the real role of every woman who has a mind and a heart: there lies her glory, and only if she plays that role will she give and find happiness.

(315)

No wonder that Turquan rises to the defense of poor Baron de Staël, Madame de Staël's first husband: "Who would not grant mitigating circumstances to that poor man, because of his wife's infernal independence?" (195).

Even though Madame de Staël might appear strong, Larg suggests "as soon as the threat becomes precise, pressing, the theoretician of perfectability abdicates and we see in her stead a poor woman, fallen to pieces, gripping the soil and fighting the active ruse of the hunter by means of the wounded animal's dull inertia" (28). Apparently unperturbed by two decades of feminist writing, Diesbach states that "of woman she has above all the obstinacy, since she is lacking in feeling and tactfulness, and also the art of mobilizing all her good qualities in the service of a character flaw" (231). One cannot entirely escape the impression that critics – both male and female – exploit their ambiguous position to the hilt. Since the "woman" strategy is designed to apologize for some aspects of Madame de Staël's character and behavior, the apology will be the stronger the more Madame de Staël can be shown to have been a woman. Consequently, critics feel free to identify her with their pet prejudices about women. Only the most recent books try to put matters in perspective. Simone Balayé writes: "in her time woman has no function outside of the family, plays no political role, has no power at all; it is therefore deemed highly unacceptable for her to manifest or publish any opinion whatsoever" (96).

There must, accordingly, be something wrong with women who do. Cousin d'Avalon quotes a certain Jesuit, Cerutti, as saying: "Madame de Staël has a plan; it becomes clear; she wants to go beyond her gender" (56). In the same book Madame de Genlis goes as far as to suggest that Madame de Staël really has no other option, since she has "man-like features and a man-like build" (40). The reason why she does not behave like a woman is not just that she wants to behave like a man, but that she was meant to be a man. Pailleron writes about her "virile brain" (147) and Larg describes her as a "virile intelligence in a body that is alas but little feminine" (80).

The third strategy of apology therefore concentrates on the education Madame de Staël was given. Sainte-Beuve gives a somewhat innocuous description of the process:

> I can almost see her in the study, under her mother's very eyes, walking up and down the room, a volume in her hand, reading the book she was obliged to read as she approached her mother's chair, and then, as she slowly walked away again, replacing it by a sentimental romance.
>
> (52)

Since Madame de Staël's mother was in charge of her education, the "woman" strategy admirably complements the "education" strategy. No wonder things went wrong. As a child Madame de Staël had to leave Paris to regain her health, thus proving "the bankruptcy of Madame Necker's [her mother's] system; she was to bear her daughter a grudge over this, since she considered her guilty of having betrayed her hopes" (Diesbach 36). The "education" strategy, in turn, ties in well with the "psychology" strategy. Once Madame Necker no longer supervises the education of her daughter, that daughter is drawn much more toward her father and Madame Necker "notices also, not without pain, that her daughter usurps by Necker's side the place and the influence that are rightfully hers" (Diesbach 41). Again, what holds true for the "woman" strategy also holds true here: the worse educated Madame de Staël can be shown to be, the stronger the apology. Critics therefore feel free to vent their views on education: "Spoiled beyond measure by her father who forbade her nothing and forgave her all her whims, by her mother who had renounced the imposition of any discipline, the little one only did what she did not dislike. She was to stay like that all her life" (Turquan 4). Again, the "woman" and "education" strategy combine in Pailleron's rather cheap remark on Madame Necker who "no doubt would have had her [Madame de Staël] translate the Apocalypse while she was cutting her first teeth" (6). Education can also be made to take the blame for the affairs Madame de Staël got embroiled in, or even for the fact that people suspect that she might have had affairs if the critic is not willing to acknowledge that she actually had them. Because the young Madame de Staël was exposed to so many intellectuals of the time and to so much intellectual conversation in her mother's salon, she became capable of developing "intellectual friendships" with many men. Yet "The intellectual friendship, which produced so many delightful friendships between herself and distinguished men of all countries, was naturally attributed, by ladies of inferior gifts, to a source less innocent" (Child 75).

Many of the French critics discussed here also tend to hold Madame de Staël's education responsible for the fact that she is either "not really" French, or not "French enough." Souriau regrets that "she no longer believes in the idea of a fatherland" (8), only to contradict himself – it will be remembered that he is the critic who accused Madame de Staël of contradicting herself, excusing her afterwards on the grounds that she was a woman – at the end of his book when he praises Madame de Staël for rallying to Napoleon during the Hundred Days: "faced with strangers, faced with enemies, one does not notice which hands hold the flag; one runs to the flag because that is where France is" (110). Pailleron, on the other hand, does not forgive Madame de Staël her earlier opposition to Napoleon: "to desire the humiliation of France, its misfortune, the sacrifice of its army is not what a French woman does. Germaine Necker was not one" (48). Whereas these sentiments may be understandable in the context of their time (Souriau published his book in 1910, Pailleron hers in 1931), they still resurface in Diesbach as late as 1984, though now aimed at Constant rather than at Madame de Staël herself: "It is rather unpleasant to see the greed with which Constant, a subject of the canton of Wallis, in Switzerland, sizes up France as a country conquered and cynically calculates all he will be able to get out of it in the field of riches and even honors" (173).

Between 1870 and 1960, to be anti-French implied of necessity that one was pro-German. The French critics of that period cavalierly allow their anti-German sentiment to intrude in all discussions of Madame de Staël's undisputed masterpiece *De l'Allemagne,* one of the seminal writings of European Romanticism.

Souriau curtly states: "This book should be read in the light of 1870 by a French-man who wants to find a topical use for even old books. Are we not right in saying that Mme de Staël was wrong and that she has misled us?" (95). In 1820 Albertine Necker de Saussure could still write the following about Madame de Staël's travels in Germany: "Men of genius, and of genius analogous to her own, received her with transport; sovereigns contended for her; and a friendly society applauded her talents, her political conduct, and her enthusiastic regard for her father" (112). In 1893 Sorel already states: "Those Germans were little concerned with the foundation of a free state and the promulgations of laws destined to shape virtuous citizens" (107). Larg, on the other hand, gives Madame de Staël some credit: she "seems to sense in advance the dangers of the imperatives of German mysticism that weigh down Fichte's *Lectures,* Schelling's *Inquiries* into freedom and Schlegel's *Course On Dramatic Poetry*" (158). In 1984 Diesbach has recourse to euphemisms to veil his evaluation of Madame de Staël's "racial" origins when he describes her reaction to Italy and the Italians: "With regard to the population Madame de Staël keeps that atavistic disdain people of the North have for people of the South" (327). Souriau is more blunt in 1910: "Mme de Staël is not totally French; she is a little Swiss, very Genevan, with a little bit of the Germanic which comes to her through her ancestors" (4).

There are some voices redressing the balance. Françoise d'Eaubonne writes that "Napoleon certainly did much more to prepare future attempts at revenge, first by humiliating the Germans and then by erecting the foundations of a national unity, than did Germaine's naiveté concerning those 'noble savages' of Europe" (195). Yet the visceral anti-German bias of French criticism in the period, combined with the traditional ethnocentric orientation of French criticism is partially responsible for the neglect in critical and historical writing of the role played by the "Coppet group," the group of cosmopolitan intellectuals gathering at Madame de Staël's mansion at Coppet in Switzerland, which included Constant, Byron, and A. W. Schlegel. They were developing and discussing both the concept and the real-ity of a "European" literature *avant la lettre.* Small wonder, then, that Pailleron, who published her book in 1931, feels she has to counteract the faddist image of Madame de Staël refurbished by the League of Nations: "they want to discover in her the promotor of that European spirit taste requires intellectuals and snobs to dress in these days" (42). The fact remains that "for a long time there have not been any studies written about the Coppet group, that has not been regarded as a literary movement by French historians. Why this gap? Probably mainly because the group is not exclusively French" (Balayé 110).

A final strategy for apology is that of the traditional hagiographies. Many a saint turns out to have been a sinner, and not of the meanest, early in his or her earthly existence, only to convert to the true faith toward the end of it. Since all is well that ends well, the sinner is forgiven and proclaimed not just a saint, but also an example for other sinners to emulate. Here again Albertine Necker de Saussure takes an early lead where she writes about the middle-aged Madame de Staël that "her independent mind, her intellect, friendly to light and acquiring it in all directions, was every day more and more convinced of the sublime truths of Christianity" (10). Sainte-Beuve echoes: "we shall see at last, at the end of this triumphal path as at the end of the most humbly pious, we shall see a cross" (94). By linking Madame de Staël's path with that of the humble Sainte-Beuve manages to redeem her from the opprobrium directed at the wealthy, the better to enroll her in his crusade for a renewed Christianity which will save France and Europe, obviously in that order, even though "the way in which Christianity will set to work to regain its hold upon the society of the future remains yet veiled" (76).

Since the saint's conversion is the more laudable the more formidable the obstacles that stand in its way, Sorel obligingly prints a catalogue of temptations and evil influences Madame de Staël was exposed to, yet managed almost miraculously to overcome:

> And there she stands, in that malicious and hostile society, exposed to all surprises and to all sophisms of the passions. Nothing defends her against them. A vague deism, the dust of a religion ruined by the sarcasms of the philosophers; a romanesque morality inclined towards all casuistry of sentiment, a marriage cold and unattractive: weak defenses against the onslaught of a corrupt world.
>
> (30)

Obviously the highest praise is due for a woman who, in spite of all of this, concludes that "there is no other philosophy than the Christian religion" (Sorel 136). The only remaining blemish appears to be that she remains, after all, a woman, and therefore *ipso facto* less amenable to logic: "If logic had still guided her, she would have gone as far as Pascal; but Pascal would have carried her too high" (Sorel 136) – he was a man, after all, and a mathematician. Later critics deny that Madame de Staël was saved by religion: "She finds less help than ever in this direction" (Larg 213). Probably because "she found the solution to her problems in herself" (Diesbach 449).

Since Staëlien criticism remains so firmly anchored in the biographical domain, it happens not infrequently that features taken from novelistic discourse enter the discourse of criticism. Sainte-Beuve, for instance, contributes the following "idyllic" description of Coppet: "it is the seclusion, the interchange of thoughts and ideas among these guests beneath the leafy shades, and the noon-day talks by the brink of these lovely waters clothed with verdure" (118). Françoise d'Eaubonne obliges with the following totally imaginary conversation between two Parisians, obviously included in her book only to give the reader a "flavor" of what such conversations "might have been like":

> – Is it true that M. de Montrond is going to fight a duel?
> – How could it be otherwise with his notoriety? Is he not the darling of all loose women?
> – In the meantime he devours his wife's fortune at the gambling table. That poor Aimée de Coigny . . .
> – What a team: "The Young Captive" and the "Christ child in Hell"!
>
> (34)

Most French Staëlien critics are, finally, not unduly troubled by considerations of accuracy, especially not where German literature is concerned. Larg writes: "Mme de Staël did not, like Goethe, have the felicitous gift of making little songs out of her great sufferings" (28). Unfortunately, the disguised quote should not be attributed to Goethe, but to Heine, the same Heine who nowhere said that "Schlegel was a-sexual" (79) as the same Larg makes him say in his own *De l'Allemagne,* written as an answer to Madame de Staël's book of the same title. Similarly, there can hardly be said to have been a "falling off, a decadence" (Sainte-Beuve 125) in German poetry after the death of Goethe.

It is, in conclusion, not easy to escape the impression that Madame de Staël has not been exceedingly well served by her French rewriters. The image of her they have projected remains tributary to that first image projected by Albertine Necker de Saussure, whether subsequent critics agree with that image or not. By not trying to transcend it, they condemn Madame de Staël's reputation to the vagaries of biographical speculation and gratuitous gossip.

12 Editing

Salvation through mutilation: Büchner's *Danton's Death*

On the run from the kind of justice he spent his short life trying to overthrow, Georg Büchner sent the manuscript of his play *Dantons Tod* (*Danton's Death*) to the then famous German novelist and essayist Karl Gutzkow. Gutzkow was known for his liberal political leanings and therefore was the obvious choice to evaluate the manuscript. Gutzkow liked the play and tried to publish it. Considering the play's content, this was not likely to prove an easy task in the repressive Germany of the 1830s. A play depicting at least some of the main characters of the French Revolution in a positive manner could not count on much official sympathy in a Germany (and Austria-Hungary) fashioned by Metternich after the 1815 Vienna Congress with the express intent of counteracting the "pernicious" influence of the Revolution.

Metternich's "Justice" had all kinds of legal means at its disposal to prevent the publication of "seditious" material. The German states were legally entitled to have recourse to "preventive censorship as well as censorship after publication, holding editors responsible for what they published, forbidding publication, deportation" (Hauschild 165). Faced with all this, Gutzkow decided to exploit his position as co-editor of the Frankfurt literary journal *Phönix*. He took advantage of the fact that the editor-in-chief was on honeymoon to publish extracts from Büchner's play in the journal.

Next, encouraged by positive reactions to the publication of these extracts, Gutzkow offered the play in its entirety to a publisher, J. D. Sauerländer. Both Gutzkow and Sauerländer realized they would have to resort to preventive censorship to get the play published at all. In Gutzkow's own words: "in order not to give the censor the pleasure of striking passages, I performed the job myself" (64). The job was neither an easy nor a pleasant one to perform. Looking back on it in his obituary on Büchner, Gutzkow described what he had to do:

> Long, ambiguous dialogues in the popular scenes, that scintillated with wit and mind games had to be left behind. The *pointes* of the puns had to be blunted or bent by auxiliary stupid phrases that had to be added. Büchner's real Danton was never published. What was published of it are poor leftovers, the ruins of a devastation.

(64–5)

Yet these "ruins," actually published in 1835, were to be the foundation of Büchner's fame, such as it was, for quite some time to come. Hebbel, his more fortunate and famous contemporary, liked the Sauerländer edition very much, and commented favorably. The Sauerländer edition was republished some years later, and it contributed greatly to keeping Büchner's name current in the literary world between 1835, the publication of a reasonably unmutilated version of the *Collected Works* in 1870, and the first successful staging of one of his plays in 1916.

Other editions were to follow Sauerländer's, among them one put together by Georg Büchner's brother, Ludwig, in 1850. This edition, announced as the edition of the "complete works," did not do much to re-establish the original text of *Danton's Death*. Hauschild judges it as follows: "the misprints have been taken out for the most part and the text of the manuscript has been restored in about twenty instances. But dozens of other instances still exhibit the same or similar 'stupid nonsense' as they did in 1835" (89).

It was not until the Franzos edition of 1870 that the "real" text of *Danton's Death* could be said to have been published, even though Franzos had restored thirteen passages that had been stricken from the manuscript by Büchner himself. But the fact that the text was now available almost as Büchner had written it still did not mean that it was performed on the stage as well. In fact, like the other plays of Büchner, *Danton's Death* remained a closet drama for a long time. It was staged for the first time in Berlin, by the two theater companies linked to the political left in 1902, but without success. Performances in Hamburg in 1910 and 1911 met with a similar fate. Only the Max Reinhardt production of 1916 in the Deutsches Theater in Berlin became the "big international success that established Büchner as a classic of the theater overnight" (Goltschnigg 27). Between 1911 and 1916, in 1913 to be precise, Rudolf Franz had published an "acting version" of *Danton's Death* in an attempt to persuade more theater companies to stage the play.

In this chapter we shall look at two editions of *Danton's Death,* the one made ready for publication by Gutzkow and the one made ready for the press by Franz. What we shall be looking at, in fact, are two rewritings, one (Gutzkow's) undertaken mainly for ideological reasons, the other (Franz's) mainly for poetological reasons. I have checked both rewritings/editions against the most widely available current (Reclam) edition, because that is likely to be the one that reaches the most contemporary readers.

A first glance at Gutzkow's edition reveals its basic underlying strategy. Gutzkow has added a lengthy subtitle: "Dramatische Bilder aus Frankreichs Schreckensherrschaft," where Büchner had simply called the play: "Ein Drama." The subtitle, "Dramatic Scenes from France's Reign of Terror," advertizes the play as "sensational" in an obvious attempt to defuse its political impact. Büchner's play becomes a warning description of what might happen in Germany if Germans were to follow the French example, while at the same time giving the German reader a vicarious thrill or two. Gutzkow sums it all up very neatly indeed in his introduction to the fragments of the play as published in *Phönix*: "our young people study the Revolution because they love freedom and yet they want to avoid the mistakes that may be committed in its service" (65). This attitude, which also makes the figure of Danton somewhat less ambiguous than the Danton Büchner had created, meshes relatively well with the official attitude of the censors themselves as described by Hauschild: "a muted, half-hearted liberalism was tolerated after all, one that pleaded for measured progress" (165).

Yet relatively few changes have been made in the text for political reasons. The vast majority of changes are intended to tone down or strike sexual allusions. Among the changes motivated by political considerations one might list the following. Where Büchner writes "gekrönte Verbrecher" [crowned criminals] (42), Gutzkow changes the noun that refers to the person of a ruler into the more abstract, neuter noun "gekröntes Verbrechen" [crowned crime] (82). Where Büchner writes that Danton is accused of having crawled, "gekrochen" (53), at the feet of miserable despots, Gutzkow, who was very aware of the power of the police of the despots of his Germany, wrote "gesessen" [sat] (104).

When general Dillon says in Büchner: "Man füttert das Volk nicht mit Leichen" [you do not feed the people corpses] (55), Gutzkow simply omits the sentence altogether. He also omits denigratory references to religion. In Büchner, Hérault, one of Danton's friends, tells Chaumette, a fellow prisoner, that he can "in Madame Momoro das Meisterstück der Natur anbeten, wenigstens hat sie dir die Rosenkränze dazu in den Leisten gelassen" [worship Nature's masterpiece in Madame Momoro; at least nature has left you the rosaries to do so in your loins] (48). Gutzkow omits the sentence altogether.

Similarly, when Marion, one of the prostitutes Danton frequents, says that it does not make much difference whether people find their pleasure in bodies ("Leibern"), images of Christ ("Christusbildern"), flowers, or children's toys (Büchner 20), Gutzkow (35) replaces "bodies" with "relics" ("Reliquien") and "images of Christ" with "living things" ("Lebendigen").

Gutzkow also deletes what may be taken to be offensive to the taste of the middle- and upper-class reader. Büchner's one reference to cancer ("Krebs") (57) is left out, as are his three references to body odor, or the stench emanating from people ("stinken") (67, 72). Similarly, the graphic details of the treatment Barrère, one of the politicians who side with Robespierre against Danton, has to undergo for syphilis (Büchner 59) are omitted. When Barrère asks his colleagues not to tell Robespierre about his predicament, they reply that Robespierre is "an impotent Freemason" (59), thus revealing the brittleness of Robespierre's support and lending credence to Danton's prediction that Robespierre will not long outlast him. Leaving out this line, as Gutzkow does, removes an important element from the structure of the play.

Deletion is also the major strategy Gutzkow uses for dealing with sexual references in Büchner's text. "Hure" (whore) is left out altogether in Gutzkow's version of the exchanges between Danton and Lacroix (71). "Zur Hure machen" [make into a whore] (71) is turned into the less offensive (because Latinate) "prostituirt" (140). Similarly, other instances of the use of "Hure" in Büchner (13, 30) are turned into the less offensive (because more archaic) "Meze" in Gutzkow (22, 56).

Büchner's cynical references to sex are consistently left out by Gutzkow. When Danton says in Büchner, with reference to the atmosphere in the part of Paris frequented by prostitutes: "Möchte man nicht drunter springen, sich die Hosen vom Leibe reißen und sich über den Hintern begatten wie die Hunde auf der Gasse?" [Do you not get the desire to jump in among them, tear off your pants and have anal sex like dogs in the street?] (33), he says absolutely nothing of the kind in Gutzkow.

Similarly, when a citizen tells the militiamen who come to arrest Danton that the time of night is the time when "perpendiculars are sticking out from under the bedclothes" (Büchner 40), Gutzkow omits the sentence. Yet Gutzkow also tries to "blunt" or "bend" the *pointes* of many a line written by Büchner. When Büchner's Danton says he wants to sneak out of life as "out of the bed of a merciful nurse" and adds that life "ist eine Hure, es treibt mit der ganzen Welt Unzucht" [is a whore, it fornicates with the whole world] (68), Gutzkow's Danton merely wants to "sneak out of a girl's room" (136).

When one of the women who have come out to watch the excution of Danton and his friends shouts at Hérault that she will have a wig made out of his beautiful hair, Büchner's Hérault replies: "Ich habe nicht genug Waldung für einen so abgeholtzten Venusberg" [I don't have enough trees for such a deforested mount of Venus] (74), Gutzkow's Hérault omits the "Venus" (147), thereby rendering the whole exchange more than a little puzzling, not to say nonsensical.

Yet Gutzkow leaves in those elements of Büchner's text that may be thought too witty for the censor to catch. Rosalie, one of the prostitutes in the play, has the following conversation with a soldier:

> Soldat: Du bist sehr spitz.
> Rosalie: Und du sehr stumpf.
> Soldat: So will ich mich an dir wetzen
> [Soldier: You are very sharp.
> Rosalie: And you are very blunt.
> Soldier: Then I want to whet myself on you.]
> (33)

Gutzkow leaves the dialogue unchanged. He also exploits every instance in which Latin words are used in Büchner's text to connote sexual innuendo, reasoning, as the censor would no doubt also have done, that they are unintelligible to the majority of the readers anyway. When Büchner has Lacroix warn Danton that "der Mons Veneris wird dein Tarpejischer Fels" [the Mons Veneris will be your Tarpeian Rock] (23) Gutzkow does not change anything, leaving in on his page 43 the Latin equivalent of what he took out in German on his page 147.

Finally, Gutzkow also rewrites some of the allusions in such a way that they still make some sense, even though they lose much of the bite Büchner had given them. Büchner's Lacroix calls the prostitutes: "Quecksilbergruben" [quarries of mercury] (21), punning on the German *Silbergrube* which can mean "silver mine" and *Quecksilber,* meaning "mercury," then the only known treatment for syphilis. The prostitutes, it is hinted, are mines in which men can find things that will make them quarry mercury. Gutzkow simply calls the prostitutes "Silbergruben" (38), merely emphasizing the mercenary aspect of their profession.

As opposed to Gutzkow, Rudolf Franz thinks that *Danton's Death* is hard to stage not because its theme could still be said to be "dangerous to the state" (1), but because the audience no longer knows the history of the French Revolution and will therefore lose the thread of the action. As a result, he has struck "every allusion and every scene that is expendable because it is merely descriptive and presupposes a more precise familiarity with the subject matter" (1). Whenever he found it hard to decide, Franz used square brackets in the text. Enclosed between them are "such parts of the dialogue that can be omitted at will" (2). Franz considers himself all the more entitled to follow this course of action because, in his words: "Büchner just threw his work on the page in haste and made use of such results of his reading as he would no doubt himself have removed again as 'anorganic' when checking the text more rigorously" (1–2).

To make Büchner's play "stageable" on the German stage of his day, Franz has turned it into a "historical drama" (he simply calls the play a "drama") in the Schillerian tradition. Since that kind of drama is much closer to the "three unities" of time, place, and action than Büchner's episodic play, itself inspired by the writings of the members of the "Storm and Stress" group, Franz has "distilled the fall of the Dantonists as briefly and as sharply as possible by reducing the 32 scenes [in Büchner] to 15. In doing so, I have given it the necessary form that will allow every serious theater company to stage it and every serious audience to respond to it" (2).

True to the Schillerian tradition, Franz's play adds many characters, painfully explicitating the "etc." in Büchner's initial list of characters. Yet Franz also omits one character altogether: that of (Thomas) Payne. Franz strikes the whole first scene of Büchner's third act, in which Payne demonstrates the non-existence of God to his fellow prisoners. The scene, which Franz no doubt interpreted as "merely descriptive" goes a long way to explain the cynical undercurrent in Büchner's play. Since the scene runs to more than three pages in the Reclam edition, Franz must also have thought that it would distract the audience's attention from the development of the plot.

Similarly Franz omits the fifth scene of Büchner's third act, which is absolutely pivotal for the plot of the whole play. In that scene, set in the prison where the prisoners of the Terror await their fate, Dillon, a general, hatches the plan to break out and gather enough soldiers to free Danton. He also suggests that Danton's and Camille Desmoulins's wives throw money to the crowds to bolster their enthusiasm for Danton's cause. Dillon is denounced by the fellow prisoner he made privy to his plan, and it is this plan that is used as evidence by the public prosecutor to accuse Danton and his friends of high treason, to convict them, and to sentence them to death. The whole scene disappears from Franz's version of the play, but the evidence surfaces nevertheless, on page 56, corresponding exactly to Büchner's page 63. The reader or spectator of Büchner's text will know where the evidence comes from. The reader or spectator of the Franz version is – literally – presented with a *coup de théâtre* rather than with Büchner's logical build-up of the action. Moreover, the cynical betrayal of the general by a fellow prisoner, one more act of cynical betrayal after many, made possible (and necessary?) by the turbulent times, is also left out of Franz's version.

In keeping with the unities, the execution of Danton and his friends is not shown on Franz's stage, though it is on Büchner's (act IV, scene 7). Also more or less in keeping with the unities, each of Franz's three acts takes place in the same location, whereas Büchner's less tightly connected scenes jump from one location to another over four acts. To achieve his "unity," Franz has to rearrange scenes and to rewrite stage directions. In the second act, for instance, Büchner's scenes 1 to 6 are all incorporated into one big scene. In the third act Büchner's scene 2 is put behind his scene 3. In the same act the "unity" of location, being the "Revolutionary Tribunal," necessitates an almost comically repeated entering and leaving the stage on the part of the major characters. Thus "The members of the jury and the accused enter" on Franz's page 48, the "judges leave" on page 50 and the "accused are led away" on page 52, only to reappear a few pages later.

The whole of Franz's second act takes place in the "street of the second scene" (30). Büchner's second act opens in "a room" (29), in which Danton "is dressing" (29). In Franz he has to "leave his house" for the audience to see him in the street. Büchner's second scene in the same act takes place on a "promenade" where "passers-by" walk about. Franz keeps this, but has his scene run on. The room where Camille and his wife, Lucille, meet with Danton in the third scene of Büchner's second act is also turned into "another part of the street." Danton's meditation on life and death, which takes place in "an empty field" in the fourth scene of Büchner's second act, takes place somewhat less convincingly on the street in Franz. The same, ubiquitous street is also the locus of the conversation between Danton and Julie, his wife, which takes place in a room in the fifth scene of Büchner's second act. Since Büchner's Danton is in a room in that scene he can, quite logically, stand "by the window" (38). Franz has to get Danton from Büchner's fourth scene in the second act to Büchner's fifth scene by means of the rather clumsy use of a not exactly plausible stage direction. Franz's Danton "falls asleep [in the street, sic]. Night has come. Suddenly he awakes with a start" (38).

In keeping with the Schillerian historical drama Franz's stage directions are also more explicit than Büchner's. Where Büchner writes "eine Gasse" [an alley] (11), Franz has "eine Strasse, Häuser, Bäume, eine Bank" [a street, houses, trees, a bench] (11). Büchner's laconic "ein Zimmer" [a room] (5, 19, 24) is turned into "ein elegantes Zimmer" [an elegant room] (7), "ein anderes Zimmer" [another room] (19), and "ein sehr einfaches Zimmer" [a very simple room] (25). Finally, to justify not showing the execution on the stage, Franz has to add the following elaborate stage direction, which is nowhere to be found in Büchner: "One hears the noise made by the people who walk past singing the Carmagnole. A shrill woman's voice shouts: 'Room, make room. My children are crying, they are hungry. I have to make them watch so they are quiet. Room!' " (65).

In keeping with his suspicions about the audience's knowledge of the history of the Revolution, Franz suggests cuts in Robespierre's first big speech (16), in Collot d'Herbois's speech (14), in Lacroix's speech (24), in Robespierre's self-justification (42, 43), and in the lines Danton says in his own defense (54). Furthermore, Franz persists in making cuts on "historical" grounds that make it much harder for the reader/spectator to understand the plot. Büchner's Hérault, for instance, says on page 6: "They want to turn us into antediluvians. Saint-Just would not mind seeing us crawl on all fours again, so that the lawyer from Arras [Robespierre] could invent little hats, school benches and a God for us according to the mechanism of the watchmaker from Geneva [Rousseau]." In doing so, he identifies at once the two camps that will play a part in the drama. The one camp consists of Robespierre and Saint-Just with their desire to take the revolution further, the other of Danton and his friends who think the revolution has gone far enough, and that it is time to stop. In Hérault's words, again: "The revolution must stop and the republic must begin" (7). Franz leaves in Hérault's first sentence on page 6, but deletes the second, thereby making the reader/spectator's task more difficult. Consciously or unconsciously, by suppressing historical details and whole scenes, Franz also refashions Danton in the mold of the Schillerian tragic hero as compared to the libertine, cynic, and politician he is in Büchner's play.

Büchner's text contains a number of references to the history of Republican Rome. It does so because the French Revolution saw, or rather, created its ancestor in Republican Rome. Common parlance of the revolutionary period was therefore larded with references like the following in Lacroix' speech: "Shout about the tyranny of the decemviri, speak of daggers, invoke Brutus" (29). Franz places these references between square brackets, indicating that they may be left out at the director's convenience, and destroying much of the local color Büchner had seen fit to include in his play. Barrère's references to Catilina and his conspiracy suffer the same fate on page 54.

Franz not only changes the order of the scenes in the play, not infrequently making things more complicated as he does so; he also omits the passage which is commonly regarded as Büchner's statement of his own poetics: the third scene of act II (35–6), in which Camille Desmoulins gives his views on the theater. Similarly, Camille's philosophical musings on life and death, voiced in prison toward the very end of the play (72), are put between square brackets in Franz's text (63–4).

Franz appears to want to streamline the action as much as possible to keep the audience's attention riveted on the stage throughout. Büchner's poetological and philosophical passages therefore become "interjections" from Franz's point of view, to be dispensed with if necessary. It is not altogether inconceivable that Franz thought the same about what he calls the "results" of Büchner's reading (1–2), namely the passages Büchner took over almost word for word from Thiers's and Mignet's histories of the French Revolution. Büchner did so out of a desire to reflect historical authenticity. Franz must have thought that authenticity impeded the flow of the action. This, in turn, may have inspired him to deplore his contemporaries' lack of knowledge of revolutionary events. He was probably happy to use this real or proclaimed "lack" as a "mandate" to omit from Büchner's text whatever he thought detracted from the main action.

Finally, Franz is also not completely happy with Büchner's cynically explicit sexual references. The "Quecksilbergruben" (21) referred to above are put between square brackets, and Danton's graphic description of canine anal intercourse (33), also referred to above, is left out altogether.

It remains to point out at the end of this brief analysis of two editions/rewritings of Büchner's *Danton's Death* that the rewriters/editors obviously did not wittingly and willingly set out to mutilate the text. They did what they did because they had no other choice. If Gutzkow had not mutilated Büchner the way he did, publication of *Danton's Death* would probably not have taken place and the whole fate of the publication and reception of this play and of Büchner's other works would have been radically different. Similarly, Franz "mutilated" the text of *Danton's Death* not because of any sadistic pleasure he may have felt in doing so, but to produce an "acting version" that was designed to help and encourage theater companies that were willing to try to stage Büchner again after the two unsuccessful productions in Berlin in 1902 and the unsuccessful productions in Hamburg in 1910 and 1911.

It is no coincidence that Franz's version was prepared for publication in 1913, the year of the centenary of Büchner's birth. The symbolism of the date was no doubt intended as an added incentive for theater companies finally to put Büchner on the stage and to keep him there. Needless to say, Franz's rewriting was only one among many that helped bring about successful productions of Büchner's theatrical oeuvre. Rewritings of another nature, such as critical articles by Gerhart Hauptmann, the leading playwright of the day, and many other literary figures connected with the theater also contributed to reach the desired goal.

The fate of Büchner's works is perhaps one of the most obvious examples of the power of rewriting and rewriters. If Gutzkow and Franz had not done what they did, we would now probably have a very different Büchner, or even no Büchner at all. An analysis of their rewritings, such as the one given here, also serves to illustrate in the most obvious manner possible the nature of "constraints" and their influence on the work of rewriters. The power of rewriters, it would seem, is always circumscribed by power of another, more obvious kind.

Notes

1 Given the non-status of Translation Studies at the time in the American academy, such an already established position would have been the only possibility to hire him. There were departmental colleagues involved in translation. A. Leslie Willson had co-founded the American Literary Translators Association in 1978 and edited the bi-lingual German literary journal *Dimension*. Christopher Middleton was a talented poet and a gifted translator. Outside the department were other scholars, such as M. R. Ghanoonparvar, a professor and translator of Persian literature, and for a time Gayatri Spivak was also at the University of Texas at Austin.

2 He co-wrote his own beginning Dutch textbook with Marian De Vooght: *Go Dutch!: A Beginning Textbook for University Students*. It was written with wit and verve in a faux film noir style following the travails of the detective Jan Raap.

3 Comparative Literature is an interdisciplinary program rather than a department at the University of Texas at Austin.

4 On polysystems theory in Translation Studies: Gentzler: 106–144.

5 One could mention several names, but I want to acknowledge one important figure in the United States who helped facilitate the dialogue across disciplines over decades and the growth of Translation Studies in the United States: Marilyn Gaddis Rose (1930–2015), who was at SUNY Binghamton where the first PhD in Translation Studies in the United States was established.

6 In assessing the state of the discipline, Snell-Hornby takes an interesting look at three different books, one from 1979 and two from 2001. Each gives an overview of the field, showing how much the field has grown, but she observes still the desire for integration and collaboration. (159–162)

7 That includes by me, now, in this very preface.

8 Pym is certainly capable of a direct rebuttal, but that is not his strategy here. Elsewhere he is more direct, addressing Lefevere as part of essentially the same groups. Cf., his 1995 article where he accuses Lefevere, for instance, of wanting to restrict translation scholarship to literary studies. (20)

9 For instance, in his essay "Composing the other" in *Postcolonial Translation*, edited by Bassnett and Trivedi.

10 Both concepts are introduced in *Constructing Cultures*, a collection of essays by Bassnett and Lefevere.

11 "Acculturating Bertolt Brecht" in *Constructing Cultures*.

12 For instance, a special issue of the journal *Target* edited by Cristina Marinetti focusing on theatre and translation (2013). Cf. her introduction on performance and performativity (307–320).

13 For example, Theo Hermans edited a two volume set entitled *Translating Others* with multiple contributions concerning non-Western thought about translation.

References

Foreword

Amit-Kochavi, Hannah. 1995. "Review of André Lefevere. *Translation, Rewriting and the Manipulation of Literary Fame.*" *Target* 7(2): 389–391.

Bassnett, Susan. 1998a. "The Translation Turn in Cultural Studies." In: Susan Bassnett and André Lefevere. *Constructing Cultures: Essays on Literary Translation.* Clevedon: Multilingual Matters, pp. 123–140.

Bassnett, Susan. 1998b. *Comparative Literature: A Critical Introduction.* 2nd edition. Oxford: Blackwell.

Bassnett, Susan and André Lefevere (eds). 1990. *Translation, History and Culture.* London: Pinter Publ.

Bassnett, Susan and André Lefevere. 1998. *Constructing Cultures: Essays on Literary Translation.* Clevedon: Multilingual Matters.

Bermann, Sandra and Catherine Porter (eds). 2014. *A Companion to Translation Studies.* Chichester: Wiley-Blackwell.

Gentzler, Edwin. 2001. *Contemporary Translation Theories.* 2nd edition. Clevendon: Multilingual Matters.

Hardin, James (ed.). 1992. *Translation and Translation Theory in Seventeenth-Century Germany.* Ed. Amsterdam and Atlanta: Rodopi.

Hermans, Theo (ed.). 1985. *The Manipulation of Literature: Studies in Literary Translation.* London: Croom Helm Ltd.

Hermans, Theo. 1994. "Review Essay: Translation between Poetics and Ideology." *Translation and Literature*, Vol. 3: 138–145.

Hermans, Theo (ed.) 2006. *Translating Others*, Vol. 1 and 2. Manchester: St. Jerome Press.

Lefevere, André. 1982. "Mother Courage's Cucumbers: Text, System and Refraction in a Theory of Literature." *MLS* 12(4): 3–20.

Lefevere, André. 1985. "Why Waste our Time on Rewrites? The Trouble with Interpretation and the Role of Rewriting in an Alternative Paradigm." *The Manipulation of Literature: Studies in Literary Translation.* Theo Hermans (ed.). London: Croom Helm Ltd, pp. 215–243.

Lefevere, André. 1992a. *Translating Literature: Practice and Theory in a Comparative Literature Context.* NY: MLA.

Lefevere, André. 1992b. *Translation, Rewriting, and the Manipulation of Literary Fame.* London/NY: Routledge.

Lefevere, André (ed). 1992c. *Translation, History, Culture: A Sourcebook.* Ed. André Lefevere. London/NY: Routledge.

Lefevere, André. 1998. "Acculturating Bertolt Brecht." In: Susan Bassnett and André Lefevere. *Constructing Cultures: Essays on Literary Translation*. Clevedon: Multilingual Matters, pp. 109–122.

Lefevere, André. 2002. "Composing the other." In: *Postcolonial Translation: Theory and Practice*. 2nd Edition. Ed. Susan Bassnett and Harish Trivedi. London/NY: Routledge, pp. 75–94.

Lefevere, André and Susan Bassnett. 1990. "Proust's Grandmother and the Thousand and One Nights. The 'Cultural Turn' in Translation Studies." In: *Translation, History and Culture*. Susan Bassnett and André Lefevere (eds). London: Pinter Publ, pp. 1–13.

Lefevere, André and Marian De Vooght. 1995. *Go Dutch!: A Beginning Textbook for University Students*. Newark: LinguaText, Ltd.

Marinetti, Cristina. 2011. "Cultural approaches." *Handbook of Translation*. Vol. 2. Yves Gambier and Luc van Doorslaer (eds). Amsterdam: John Benjamins Publ. Co., pp. 26–30.

Marinetti, Cristina. 2013 "Translation and Theatre: From Performance to Performativity." *Target* 25(3): 307–320.

Munday, Jeremy. 2012. *Introduction to Translation Studies*. 3rd edition. London/NY: Routledge.

Pym, Anthony. *Exploring Translation Theories*. 2nd edition. London/NY: Routledge, 2014.

Pym, Anthony. 1995. "European Translation Studies, une science qui dérange, and Why Equivalence Needn't Be a Dirty Word" *TTR : traduction, terminologie, rédaction*, 8(1): 153–176.

Snell-Hornby, Mary. 1990. "Linguistic Transcoding or Cultural Transfer? A Critique of Translation Theory in Germany." *Translation, History and Culture*. Susan Bassnett and André Lefevere (eds). London: Pinter Publ, pp. 79–86.

Snell-Hornby, Mary. 2006. *The Turns of Translation Studies*. Amsterdam: John Benjamin's Publ.

Venuti, Lawrence (ed.). 2004. *The Translation Studies Reader*. 2nd Edition. London/NY: Routledge.

1 Prewrite

Augustinus, Aurelius (St Augustine). *On Christian Doctrine*. New York: Liberal Arts Press, 1958.

Bartels, Adolf. *Geschichte der deutschen Literatur*. Braunschweig, Berlin, Hamburg: Bestermann, 1943.

Cohen, Ralph. "Introduction." *The Future of Literary Theory*. Ed. Ralph Cohen. London and New York: Routledge, 1989. vii–xx.

Dorfman, D. *Blake in the Nineteenth Century*. London and New Haven: Yale University Press, 1969.

Fitzgerald, Edward. "Letter to E. B. Crowell." *The Variorum and Definitive Edition of the Poetical and Prose Writings*. Vol. 6. New York: Doubleday, 1902.

Golding, Alan C. "A History of American Poetry Anthologies." *Canons*. Ed. Robert von Hallberg. Chicago: University of Chicago Press, 1984. 279–308.

Hillis Miller, J. "Presidential Address 1986. The Triumph of Theory, the Resistance to Reading, and the Question of the Material Base." *Publications of the Modern Language Association* 102 (1987): 281–91.

Johnson, Barbara. *A World of Difference*. Baltimore and London: Johns Hopkins University Press, 1987.

Morson, Gary Saul. "Introduction: Literary History and the Russian Experience." *Literature and History*. Ed. Gary Saul Morson. Stanford: Stanford University Press, 1986. 1–30.

Scholes, Robert. *Textual Power.* New Haven and London: Yale University Press, 1985.

Warnke, Frank. "The Comparatist's Canon." *The Comparative Perspective on Literature.* Ed. Clayton Koelb and Susan Noakes. Ithaca and London: Cornell University Press, 1988. 48–56.

2 The system: patronage

"Archipoeta." *Lateinische Lyrik des Mittelalters.* Ed. Paul Klopsch. Stuttgart: Reclam, 1985.

Belsey, Catherine. *Critical Practice.* London and New York: Methuen, 1981.

Bennett, H. S. *English Books and Readers.* Vol. 1. Cambridge: Cambridge University Press, 1952. 4 vols.

Forster, Leonard. *The Poets' Tongues.* Cambridge: Cambridge University Press, 1970.

Foucault, Michel. *Power/Knowledge.* Ed. Colin Garden. New York: Pantheon, 1980.

Gibb, H. A. R. and Landau, J. M. *Arabische Literaturgeschichte.* Zürich: Artemis, 1973.

Glasenapp, Helmut von. *Die Literaturen Indiens.* Stuttgart: Kröner, 1958.

Gutzkow, Karl. "Nachruf." *Gutzkows Werke.* Vol. 11. Ed. Reinhold Gensel. 1912. Hildesheim and New York: Georg Olms, 1974. 15 vols.

Jameson, Fredric. *The Prison House of Language.* Princeton: Princeton University Press, 1974.

Kavanagh, James H. "Shakespeare in Ideology." *Alternative Shakespeares.* Ed. John Drakakis. London: Methuen, 1985. 144–65.

Lyotard, François. *The Postmodern Condition. A Report on Knowledge.* Tr. Geoff Bennington and Brian Massumi. Minneapolis: University of Minnesota Press, 1985.

Martindale, Colin. "The Evolution of English Poetry." *Poetics* 7 (1978): 231–48.

Schmidt, Siegfried J. " 'Empirische Literaturwissenschaft' as Perspective." *Poetics* 8 (1979): 557–68.

Schwanitz, Dieter. "Systems Theory and the Environment of Theory." *The Current in Criticism.* Ed. Clayton Koelb and Virgil Lokke. Lafayette: Purdue University Press, 1987. 265–92.

Steiner, Peter. *Russian Formalism.* Ithaca and London: Cornell University Press, 1984.

Tompkins, Jane. *Sensational Designs.* New York: Oxford University Press, 1985.

Weber, Samuel. *Institution and Interpretation.* Minneapolis: University of Minnesota Press, 1987.

White, Hayden. *The Content of the Form.* Baltimore and London: Johns Hopkins University Press, 1987.

Whiteside, T. "Onward and Upward with the Arts." *The New Yorker* September 29, 1980: 48–100.

3 The system: poetics

Abd el Jalil, J. M. *Histoire de la littérature arabe.* Paris: Maisonneuve, 1960.

Baldick, Chris. *The Social Mission of English Criticism.* Oxford: Oxford University Press, 1983.

Bombaci, A. *Storia della letteratura turca.* Milan: Nuova Academia, 1956.

Browning, Robert. "The Agamemnon of Aeschylus." *The Poetical Works of Robert Browning.* New York: Macmillan, 1937.

Coseriu, Eugenio. *Textlinguistik.* Tübingen: Gunter Narr, 1981.

Eagleton, Terry. *Literary Theory.* Minneapolis: University of Minnesota Press, 1983.

Eibl, Karl. *Kritisch-rationale Literaturwissenschaft.* Munich: Fink, 1976.

Genette, Gérard. *Introduction à l'architexte.* Paris: Editions du Seuil, 1979.

Goethe, Johann Wolfgang. "Goethe." *Translating Literature: The German Tradition.* Ed. and trans. André Lefevere. Assen: Van Gorcum, 1977. 38–41.

Homberger, E., ed. *Ezra Pound. The Critical Heritage.* London: Longman, 1972.

Klopsch, Paul. "Die mittellateinische Lyrik." *Lyrik des Mittelalters.* Ed. Heinz Bergner. Vol. 1: 19–196. Stuttgart: Reclam, 1983. 2 vols.

Miner, Earl. "On the Genesis and Development of Literary Systems, I." *Critical Inquiry* 5 (1978): 339–54.

Musset, Alfred de. "Un spectacle dans un fauteuil: Namouna." *Premières Poésies.* Ed. F. Baldensperger and Robert Doré. Paris: Conard, 1922. 389–441.

Schlegel, August Wilhelm. "A. W. Schlegel." *Translating Literature: The German Tradition.* Ed. and trans. André Lefevere. Assen: Van Gorcum, 1977. 51–5.

Scholes, Robert. *Structuralism in Literature.* New Haven and London: Yale University Press, 1975.

4 Translation: the categories

Aristophanes. The Eleven Comedies. London: The Athenian Society, 1912.

Coulon, Victor and van Daele, Hilaire, eds. *Aristophane.* Paris: Les Belles Lettres, 1958.

Dickinson, Patrick. *Aristophanes.* London: Oxford University Press, 1970.

Fitts, Dudley. *Lysistrata.* New York: Harcourt, Brace, 1954.

Hadas, Moses, ed. *The Complete Plays of Aristophanes.* New York: Bantam Books, 1962.

Harrison, T. W. and Simmons, J. *Aikin Mata. The Lysistrata of Aristophanes.* Ibadan: Oxford University Press, 1966.

Hickie, W. J. *The Comedies of Aristophanes.* London: Bell, 1902.

Housman, L. *Lysistrata.* London: The Woman's Press, 1911.

Lindsay, Jack. *Lysistrata.* Garden City, NY: Halcyon House, 1950.

Maine, J. P., ed. *The Plays of Aristophanes.* Vol. 1. London: Dent; New York: Dutton, 1909. 2 vols.

Parker, Douglass. *Lysistrata.* Ann Arbor: University of Michigan Press, 1964.

Rogers, Benjamin B. *The Comedies of Aristophanes.* London: Bell, 1911.

Seldes, Gilbert. *Aristophanes' Lysistrata.* New York: Farrar and Rinehart, 1938.

Sommerstein, Alan H. *Aristophanes. The Acharnians. The Clouds. Lysistrata.* Harmondsworth: Penguin Books, 1972.

Sutherland, D. *Lysistrata.* San Francisco: Chandler Publishing Company, 1961.

Way, A. S. *Aristophanes.* London: Macmillan, 1934.

Wheelwright, C. A. *The Comedies of Aristophanes.* Oxford: Talboys, 1837.

5 Translation: ideology

Caren, Tylia and Lombard, Suzanne, trans. *Le Journal d'Anne Frank.* Paris: Calmann-Lévy, 1950.

Mooyaart-Doubleday, B. M., trans. *The Diary of Anne Frank.* London: Pan Books, 1954.

Paape, Harry *et al.,* eds. *De dagboeken van Anne Frank.* Gravenhage and Amsterdam: Staatsuitgeverij and Bert Bakker, 1986.

Schütz, Anneliese, trans. *Das Tagebuch der Anne Frank.* Frankfurt am Main: Fischer, 1955.

6 Translation: poetics

Arberry, Arthur J., trans. *The Seven Odes*. London: Allen and Unwin; New York: Macmillan, 1957.

Blunt, Wilfred Scrawen, trans. *The Seven Golden Odes of Pagan Arabia*. London: The Chiswick Press, 1903.

Cambridge History of Arabic Literature. Ed. A. F. L. Beeston and Julia Asthiany. Vol. 1. Cambridge: Cambridge University Press, 1983.

Carlyle, Joseph D., ed. and trans. *Specimens of Arabian Poetry*. London: Cadell and Davies, 1810.

Filshtinksy, I. M. *Arabic Literature*. Moscow: Nauta, 1966.

Fitzgerald, Edward. *The Variorum and Definitive Edition of the Poetical and Prose Writings*. New York: Doubleday, 1902. 7 vols.

Gibb, H. A. R. *Arabic Literature*. Oxford: Clarendon Press, 1963.

Hamori, Andreas. *On the Art of Medieval Arabic Literature*. Princeton: Princeton University Press, 1974.

Huart, Clement. *A History of Arabic Literature*. Beirut: Khayats Reprint, 1966.

Johnson, F. E. *The Seven Poems Suspended in the Temple at Mecca*. Bombay: Education Society, 1893.

Jones, Sir William. *The Works of Sir William Jones*. Delhi: Agam Prakashan Reprint, 1980. 17 vols.

Kritzeck, James, ed. *Anthology of Islamic Literature*. New York: Holt, Rinehart, and Winston, 1964. San Francisco: Meridian Books, 1975.

Lichtenstadter, Ilse. *An Introduction to Classical Arabic Literature*. New York: Twayne, 1974. New York: Schocken Books, 1975.

Lyall, Charles J., ed. and trans. *Translations of Ancient Arabian Poetry*. New York: Columbia University Press, 1930.

Nicholson, R. A. *Translations of Eastern Poetry and Prose*. Cambridge: Cambridge University Press, 1922.

——— *A Literary History of the Arabs*. Cambridge: Cambridge University Press, 1930.

Polk, W. R., ed. and trans. *The Golden Ode by Labid Ibn Rabiah*. Chicago and London: Chicago University Press, 1974.

Tuetey, Charles, ed. and trans. *Classical Arabic Poetry*. London: Kegan Paul International, 1985.

Wilson, Epiphanius, ed. *Oriental Literature: The Literature of Arabia*. New York: P. F. Collier and Son, 1900. Freeport, NY: Books for Libraries Press, 1971.

7 Translation: Universe of Discourse

Barbin, Claude. *L'Iliade d'Homère*. Paris, 1682.

Bitaubé, P. *Oeuvres d'Homère*. Paris: Tenré, 1822. 2 vols.

Cowper, William. *The Iliad and Odyssey of Homer*. Boston: Buckingham, 1814.

Dacier, Anne. *L'Iliade d'Homère*. Paris, 1713. 3 vols.

——— *Des causes de la corruption du goût*. Paris, 1714.

De la Motte, Houdar. *Oeuvres Complètes*. 1754. Geneva: Slatkine, 1970.

Hobbes, Thomas. *The Iliads and Odysses of Homer*. London, 1714.

Macpherson, James. *The Iliad of Homer*. Dublin: Thomas Ewing, 1773. 2 vols.

Ozell, John, Brown, William, and Oldsworth, William. *The Iliad of Homer*. London, 1714.

Rochefort, M. *L'Iliade d'Homère*. Paris, 1772.

Roscommon. "Essay on Translated Verse." *English Translation Theory*. Ed. T. R. Steiner. Assen: Van Gorcum, 1975.

Wood, Robert. *An Essay on the Original Genius of Homer*. Hildesheim and New York: Georg Olms, 1976.

8 Translation: language

Aiken, W. A., ed. and trans. *The Poems of Catullus*. New York: Dutton, 1950.

Copley, Frank O. *Gaius Valerius Catullus. The Complete Poetry*. Ann Arbor: The University of Michigan Press, 1957.

Goold, Charles. *Catullus*. London: Duckworth, 1983.

Gregory, Horace. *The Poems of Catullus*. New York: Norton, 1956.

Hull, William. *The Catullus of William Hull*. Calcutta: Lake Gardens Press, 1968.

Kelly, W. K. *The Poems of Catullus and Tibullus*. London: Bell, 1906.

Lindsay, Jack. *Gaius Valerius Catullus*. London: Fanfrolico, 1929.

Martin, Theodore. *The Poems of Catullus*. Edinburgh and London: Blackwood and Sons, 1875.

Michie, James. *The Poems of Catullus*. New York: Random House, 1969.

Quinn, Kenneth, ed. *Catullus. The Poems*. London: St Martin's Press, 1977.

Raphael, Frederic and McLeish, K. *The Poems of Catullus*. London: Jonathan Cape, 1978.

Sesar, Carl. *Selected Poems of Catullus*. New York: Mason and Lipscomb, 1974.

Sisson, C. H. *Catullus*. London: McGibbon and Kee, 1966.

Swanson, R. A. *Odi et Amo*. Boston: The Liberal Arts Press, 1959.

Symons-Jeune, J. F. *Some Poems of Catullus*. London: Heinemann, 1923.

Toury, Gideon. *In Search of a Theory of Translation*. Tel Aviv: The Porter Institute for Poetics and Semiotics, 1980.

Tremenheere, J. H. A. *The Lesbia of Catullus*. London: Fisher and Unwin, 1897.

Vannerem, Mia and Snell-Hornby, Mary. "Die Szene hinter dem Text: 'scenes-and-frames semantics' in der Übersetzung." *Übersetzungswissenschaft – eine Neuorientierung*. Ed. Mary Snell-Hornby. Tübingen: Francke, 1986. 184–204.

Way, A. S. *Catullus and Tibullus in English Verse*. London: Macmillan, 1936.

Whigham, Peter. *The Poems of Catullus*. Harmondsworth: Penguin Books, 1966.

Wright, F. A. *Catullus*. London: Routledge; and New York: Dutton, n.d.

Zukofsky, Celia and Louis. *Catullus*. London: Cape Goliard Press, 1969.

9 Historiography

Baekelmans, Lode. *W. G. van Focquenbroch. Een keus uit zijn werk*. Antwerpen/'s Gravenhage: Victor Resseler/M. Hols, 1911.

Bogaert, Abraham. *Willem van Focquenbroch. Alle de Werken*. Amsterdam: De Weduwe van Gijsbert de Groot, 1696.

Brandt Corstius, J. C. *Geschiedenis van de Nederlandse literatuur*. Utrecht/Antwerpen: Het Spectrum, 1959.

Calis, Piet. *Onze literatuur tot 1916*. Amsterdam: Meulenhoff, 1983.

Dangez, Herman. *Onze letterkunde*. Kapellen: De Sikkel, 1975.

Decorte, Bert. *Willem Godschalk van Focquenbroch. De geurige zanggodin*. Hasselt: Heideland, 1966.

de Gooijer, H. "Een miskend dichter." *Vaderlandsche Letteroefeningen* (1868): 353–72.

de Swaen, Michiel. *Werken van Michiel de Swaen.* Antwerpen: De Sikkel, 1928.

de Vooys, C. G. N. and Stuiveling, G. *Schets van de Nederlandse Letterkunde.* Groningen: Wolters-Noordhoff, 1980.

Everts, W. *Geschiedenis der Nederlandsche Letteren.* Amsterdam: C. L. van Langenhuysen, 1901.

Frederiks, J. G. and van den Branden, F. Jos. *Biographisch woordenboek der Noord-en Zuidnederlandsche Letterkunde.* Amsterdam: L. J. Veen, 1888.

Hermans, W. F. *Focquenbroch. Bloemlezing uit zijn lyriek.* Amsterdam: Van Oorschot, 1946.

Hofdijk, W. J. *Geschiedenis der Nederlandsche Letterkunde.* Amsterdam: Kraaij, 1872.

Kalff, G. *Geschiedenis der Nederlandsche Letterkunde.* Groningen: Wolters, 1909.

Kobus, J. C. and de Rivecourt, Jhr. W. *Biographisch woordenboek van Nederland.* Arnhem/Nijmegen: Gebroeders E. en M. Cohen, 1886.

Kuik, C. J. *Bloemlezing uit de gedichten en brieven van Willem Godschalk van Focquenbroch.* Zutphen: Thieme, 1977.

Langendijk, Pieter. *De Gedichten van Pieter Langendijk.* Amsterdam, 1721.

Lodewick, H. J. M. F., Coenen, P. J. J., and Smulders, A. A. *Literatuur. Geschiedenis en Bloemlezing.* Den Bosch: Malmberg, 1985.

Moderne Encyclopedie der Wereldliteratuur. Hilversum: Paul Brand en C. de Boer Jr., 1965.

Moderne Encyclopedie der Wereldliteratuur. Haarlem/Antwerpen: De Haan/Standaard Boekhandel, 1980.

Ornee, W. A. and Wijngaards, N. C. H. *Letterkundig Kontakt.* Zutphen: Thieme, 1971.

Prinsen, J. *Handboek tot de Nederlandsche Letterkundige Geschiedenis.* 's Gravenhage: Nijhoff, 1920.

Rens, Lieven. *Acht Eeuwen Nederlandse Letteren.* Antwerpen/Amsterdam: De Nederlandsche Boekhandel, 1975.

Roose, Lode. *En is 't de liefde niet.* Leiden: Sijthoff, 1971.

Schenkeveld-van der Dussen, M. A. "Focquenbroch's recalcitrante poëtica." *Traditie en Vernieuwing.* Ed. W. J. van den Akker, G. J. Dorleijn, J. J. Kloek, and L. H. Mosheuvel. Utrecht/Antwerpen: Veen, 1985.

Ter Laan, K. *Letterkundig Woordenboek voor Noord en Zuid.* 's Gravenhage/Djakarta: Van Goor, 1952.

Te Winkel, J. *De ontwikkelingsgang der Nederlandsche Letterkunde.* Haarlem: Erven F. Bohn, 1924.

van Bork, G. J. and Verkruijsse, P. *De Nederlandse en Vlaamse Auteurs.* Haarlem: De Haan, 1985.

van der Aa, A. J. *Biographisch Woordenboek der Nederlanden.* 's Gravenhage: Nijhoff, 1859.

van Heerikhuizen, F. W. *Spiegel der eeuwen.* Rotterdam: W. L. en J. Brusse, 1949.

Witsen Geysbeek, P. G. *Biographisch, anthologisch en critisch woordenboek der neder-duitsche dichters.* Amsterdam: C. L. Schleijer, 1882.

Worp, J. A. "Focquenbroch." *De Gids* (1881): 499–532.

10 Anthology

Allen, Samuel, ed. *Poems from Africa.* New York: Thomas Y. Crowell, 1973.

Chevrier, Jacques. *Littérature nègre.* Paris: Armand Colin, 1974.

Hughes, Langston, ed. *Poems from Black Africa.* Bloomington: Indiana University Press, 1963.

Kgositsile, Keorapetse, ed. *The Word Is Here.* New York: Doubleday, 1973.

Moore, Gerald and Beier, Ulli, eds. *Modern Poetry from Africa.* Harmondsworth: Penguin Books, 1963.

Moore, Gerald and Beier, Ulli, eds. *Modern Poetry from Africa*. Harmondsworth: Penguin Books, 1968.

Moore, Gerald and Beier, Ulli, eds. *Modern African Poetry*. Harmondsworth: Penguin Books, 1984.

Okpewho, Isidore, ed. *The Heritage of African Poetry*. London: Longman, 1985.

Reed, John and Wake, Clive, eds. *A Book of African Verse*. London: Heinemann, 1964.

Reed, John and Wake, Clive, eds. *A New Book of African Verse*. London: Heinemann, 1984.

Senanu, K. E. and Vincent, T., eds. *A Selection of African Poetry*. London: Longman, 1976.

Sergeant, Howard, ed. *African Voices*. New York: Lawrence Hill, 1973.

Soyinka, Wole, ed. *Poems of Black Africa*. London: Secker and Warburg, 1975.

11 Criticism

Balayé, Simone. *Madame de Staël*. Paris: Klincksieck, 1979.

Child, Maria L. *Memoirs of Madame de Staël and of Madame Roland*. Auburn: Littlefield, 1861.

Cousin d'Avalon, Victor. *Staëliana*. Paris: Librairie Politique, 1820.

D'Eaubonne, Françoise. *Une Femme témoin de son siècle*. Paris: Flammarion, 1966.

Diesbach, Ghislain de. *Madame de Staël*. Paris: Perrin, 1984.

Larg, David. *Madame de Staël*. New York: Knopf, 1926.

Necker de Saussure, Albertine. *Sketch of the Life, Character, and Writings of Baroness de Staël-Holstein*. London: Treuttel and Würtz, 1820.

Pailleron, Marie-Louise. *Madame de Staël*. Paris: Hachette, 1931.

Sainte-Beuve, The Essays of. Ed. W. Sharp. London and Philadelphia: Gibbings and Lippincott, 1901.

Sorel, Albert. *Madame de Staël*. Paris: Hachette, 1893.

Souriau, Maurice. *Les Idées morales de Madame de Staël*. Paris: Bloud, 1910.

Turquan, Joseph. *Madame de Staël. Sa vie amoureuse, politique et mondaine*. Paris: Emile Paul, 1926.

Vallois, Marie-Claire. *Fictions féminines*. Stanford: French and Italian Studies, 1987.

12 Editing

Büchner, Georg. *Dantons Tod. Dramatische Bilder aus Frankreichs Schreckensherrschaft*. Frankfurt am Main: Sauerländer, 1835.

Büchner, Georg. *Dantons Tod*. Stuttgart: Reclam, 1974.

Franz, Rudolf. *Dantons Tod. Ein Drama in 3 Akten (15 Bildern) von Georg Büchner*. Munich: Birk, 1913.

Goltschnigg, Dietmar. "Überblick über die Rezeptions- und Wirkungsgeschichte Büchners." *Materialien zur Rezeptions- und Wirkungsgeschichte Georg Büchners*. Ed. Dietmar Goltschnigg. Kronberg am Taurus: Skriptor, 1974. 9–45.

Gutzkow, Karl. "Georg Büchner: Dantons Tod." *Phönix. Frühlingszeitschrift für Deutschland* Nr 162 (July 11, 1835). Quoted in *Materialien zur Rezeptions- und Wirkungsgeschichte Georg Büchners*. Ed. Dietmar Goltschnigg. Kronberg am Taurus: Skriptor, 1974. 63–6.

Gutzkow, Karl. "Nachruf." *Gutzkows Werke*. Ed. Reinhold Gensel. Hildesheim and New York: Georg Olms, 1974, 15 vols. 11: 80–90.

Hauschild, Jan-Christoph. *Georg Büchner*. Königstein am Taurus: Athenäum, 1985.

Index

Printed in Great Britain
by Amazon

26594634R00084